Secret Churches

Secret Churches

Richard Surman

Collins

Collins, a division of HarperCollins*Publishers*
77–85 Fulham Palace Road, London W6 8JB

www.collins.co.uk

First published in Great Britain in 2008 by HarperCollins*Publishers*

1

Text copyright © Richard Surman 2008
Photography copyright © HarperCollins Publishers
Sketches and maps by Keturah Dodd © HarperCollins Publishers

Richard Surman asserts the moral right to be identified as the author
and photographer of this work.

A catalogue record for this book is available from the British Library.

ISBN-13 978-0-00-725185-8

Printed and bound in Hong Kong

Contents

Introduction

On the banks of Loch Awe is one of the most extraordinary churches in the British Isles, built by an amateur architect and avid collector, Walter Campbell. The architecture is an eccentric and bizarre mixture of Romanesque, Celtic, Italianate and Gothic: it is filled with exaggerated sculptures, and every corner reveals a surprise; its exterior is a mass of spires, turrets and buttresses, with downspouts in the form of frantic hares struggling out of the stonework, and solemn faux-Celtic owls gazing down from the balustrades. This church – St Conan's Kirk – was built so that Walter Campbell's elderly mother would not have far to travel to get to church. What is fascinating about it is that it dramatically transcends its original purpose. Constructed for an eminently practical reason, St Conan's Kirk became, over the years, a place of strange beauty and spiritual atmosphere in a landscape of outstanding beauty.

My interest in churches was first awakened by a Benedictine lay brother, the art master at my boarding school in Herefordshire. We tramped the countryside sketching landscapes, and our first walk took us to Kilpeck, with its tiny, richly carved Romanesque church dedicated to St Mary and St David, and thence to the truncated Cistercian splendour of Holy Trinity and St Mary at Abbey Dore (in the 1950s in a state of considerable neglect). The impact that the dramatic contrast between the two churches had on me never diminished, although for a few years it lay fallow, awoken again when the same lay brother sent me a battered but much appreciated copy of Cox and Ford's *The Parish Churches of England*, together with a letter in which he asked if I still remembered, 'How we crunched, exhausted but exhilarated, through frosty fields under a starry Herefordshire sky, after a twenty-mile walk to sketch the little church at Kilpeck.' This had been an essentially romantic introduction, in which the church was an element of beauty in the landscape; it was only later, when I started to go into churches that I realised there was so much more to discover – a heady mixture of setting, architecture, history, religious and social life – elements that encapsulate the remarkable living heritage of Christianity in Britain. For years my work as a landscape photographer gave me the opportunity to wander the length and breadth of the British Isles, during the course of which I came across more and more churches – some magnificent, some humble, all equally interesting for different reasons – but it was the parish churches that really caught my attention. These are churches rooted in their communities, whose buildings reflect wealth, poverty, patronage, humble endeavour, social change and political upheaval.

To get to know some of these churches is to appreciate the reasons for change, be it the impact of the Gothic arch – an astounding engineering achievement whose aesthetic impact has shaped church architecture since the 13th century – the seismic impact of the Reformation, or the return to 'sacramental' liturgy in the Church of England brought about by the Oxford Movement in the 19th century. In all cases, churches reflect the activities, beliefs, attitudes and fashions, and the technical competences of the communities within which they exist. There are several elements to be experienced in a church: the physical setting, the spiritual and liturgical, the aesthetic, the social and historical.

Firstly, the setting: why is a church built in a particular place? In many instances the church that we see is not as it was when originally built. Take, for example, St Anne's Church in Ancroft, near the border between Northumberland and Scotland. The village that it served is all but gone, burnt down after the plague swept through. All that remains is a series of mounds to indicate the site of the old village. The tower of the church was a later addition, built not to house bells, but rather to provide a secure refuge in times of civil unrest. In complete contrast, the Church of St Thomas à Becket, floating gently in the isolation of the Romney Marshes, served a scattered rural population, and the landscape in which it sits is much as it was a thousand years ago. The quest for monastic remoteness also brought with it other incidental qualities: Pluscarden Abbey is in a setting of exquisite beauty, but the site was not chosen for beauty, rather for its remoteness and its detachment from the distractions of the worldly.

The Friends Meeting House in Coanwood illustrates for me two particular elements: setting and spirituality. Despite the 1689 Toleration Act, which permitted liberty of religious worship, Quakers were still regarded in many quarters as 'strange', and remained subject to laws restricting access to universities and public office, so many meeting houses were built in out-of-the way places. This Friends Meeting House is such a place: the stark beauty of its setting is a consequence of the quest for privacy. There is also a deep sense of spiritual peace inside: the interior eschews decoration and ornamentation; it is plain, dignified and curiously welcoming.

There are extreme contrasts that reflect differences in liturgy too: the High Church interior of St Barnabas's in London's Pimlico is a perfect expression of the Oxford Movement's Anglo-Catholic missionary zeal. The intriguing, if rather cheerless, interior of Cromarty East Church is an excellent example of a post-Reformation church interior, as is Walpole Old Chapel in Suffolk. Ecumenism finds its highest expression in the interior arrangements of St Dunstan-in-the-West in London, with side altars dedicated to many different Christian traditions.

The aesthetic element is best seen in Marc Chagall's stained-glass memorial windows at All Saints' in Tudeley, and Laurence Whistler's etched glass windows at St Nicholas's in Moreton. These are outstanding examples of contemporary church art.

Nowhere could the social element of a church building be better illustrated than at the Watts Cemetery Chapel in Compton. This chapel was born of the Victorian idealism of the Home Arts and Industries Association, a noble enterprise undertaken by villagers under the tuition of Mary Watts, wife of the Victorian painter and sculptor George Frederic Watts. And, in a different way, so the Church of the Most Holy Trinity at Blythburgh reflects a social dimension in church architecture – it is a breathtaking example of the Perpendicular, eloquently expressing the wealth and pious intentions of the church's patrons.

There is one more dimension that fascinates me: the idiosyncratic and the quirky historical human touch. All too often one's senses can be almost overwhelmed by the grandeur of a church, making it easy to overlook the fact that all churches are built by, and are used by, ordinary people. These people leave their mark too, on a much more intimate level, either in the fabric of the building, or perhaps in records and diaries. Masons' marks were made, not for posterity, but to ensure that the individual mason got paid correctly. Graffiti, scratched into stonework, is a permanent unofficial record of someone's transitory presence. The mechanical hand in the organ loft at Ripon cathedral was installed to solve a problem of communication between organist and choir. And, in a completely different vein, what better commentary on church life could there be than the acerbic journal entries of William Bulkeley – squire, diarist and congregation member of St Mechell, a small Anglesey church at Llanfechell – pulling to pieces the sermons of the poor incumbent rector.

My criteria for choosing these entries include whether a church is not widely known, whether there is some feature that is not widely known or is unexpected, and whether there may be something about a particular church that, although known, still comes as a complete surprise to the first-time visitor. These features are many, and varied: in the case of St Nicholas's in Moreton, it is the etched glass windows; at St Magnus's in Kirkwall it is the upper levels of the cathedral, recently opened to energetic visitors; at Llangefni's St Cwyfan's on the Isle of Anglesey, it is simply the incredible setting; while St Bega's, on the shores of Bassenthwaite Lake, has been included for its simple architectural charm, as well as its beautiful lakeside setting. Other churches have been included for their associations with people or events: the Italian Chapel at Lambholm on the Orkney Islands for the moving story of the collaboration between the Italian prisoner of war Domenico Chiocchetti and the camp commandant; and St John's Church in Largs is the only building ever designed by the promising young Scottish architect Archibald Grahame – it is Victorian Byzantine set in bed-and-breakfast territory.

I have neither attempted to rate churches, nor do I claim that the churches featured here represent the 'best'. Others have done that exceptionally well. This is my personal selection. I have tried to link churches that are close to each other, so that the reader may find it easier to combine visits to a number of churches. England is divided into five sections: Northern England, Western England, Central and Eastern England, London and Southeast England, and Southwest England. There are undoubtedly gaps in the physical distribution of the churches featured. To some extent that reflects the distribution of churches on the ground, and to some extent it reflects my own preferences; I make no apology for the preponderance of Herefordshire churches in the Western England section, for it is these churches that so vividly captured my adolescent imagination.

In Ireland and Scotland I have featured a number of ruined churches and abbeys. The fact is that churches in Ireland suffered much more from the unwelcome attentions of either the invading Danes, the English, or warring factions within Ireland, and, as such, the resulting ruined churches are a much more dominant feature of the ecclesiastical landscape. To a lesser extent the same applies in Scotland: Norse incursions, the invading English, the impact of the Reformation, and the Highlands land clearances, all had an impact on the church 'landscape'.

Throughout the British Isles, church attendance is currently in dramatic decline, and this book pays tribute to the determination of the many people who struggle against the odds to maintain their churches, keeping them open, clean and welcoming. Where there has been redundancy, a number of voluntary organisations have stepped in. Churches restored and maintained by the excellent Friends of Friendless Churches (FOFC) feature widely in the Wales section, as do churches in England that are supported and cared for by the equally admirable Churches Conservation Trust (CCT). Smaller organisations also contribute invaluable support – the Historic Chapels Trust (HCT) and Scottish Redundant Churches Trust (SRCT) are two such. One must acknowledge too the support of official government bodies: in Wales CADW has done much to preserve the ecclesiastical landscape, as has the Office of Public Works (OPW) in Ireland, whose approach is an interesting one, quite different from that of the official conservation bodies in England, and I deal with this in the separate introduction to Ireland. Historic Scotland (HS) plays a pivotal part in the preservation of churches throughout Scotland, maintaining around 22 churches.

My sources have been many, but in particular I'd like to acknowledge the writers and compilers of church guides, many of which are very scholarly and well-informed. I have used some archaic books as well as contemporary ones for source material. Cox and Ford's *The Parish Churches of England*, and Cox and Vallance's *English Church Fittings, Furniture, and Accessories* are old companions of mine, as are many of the excellent Shell Guide series. The Pevsner 'Buildings of England' series is of course invaluable, and mention must be made of Simon Jenkins' outstanding book on *England's Thousand Best Churches*. I have used other sources too, and of these I single out Simon Knott's outstanding websites on the churches of Suffolk and Norfolk, informed and well-written labours of love.

I am extremely grateful to Ian Metcalfe at Collins Reference, whose enthusiastic interest, support and patience has made the book possible, and to his assistant Ruth Roff, for her support and attention to detail and organisation. Kirstie Addis's eagle-eyed copy-editing has been invaluable, reining in my more florid outbursts, and providing invaluable feedback regarding dates, names and technical points. Of the many helpful and welcoming vicars, churchwardens and volunteers that I encountered during the course of my wanderings, I'd like especially to mention Trevor Salmon, an enthusiastic member of the Friends of Friendless Churches, who took me around Anglesey, and whose many suggestions steered me to some of the most interesting of the Welsh churches; Erick Mayhew, the church warden at St Helen's in Kelloe; Father Gerry at St Gregory's in Preshome, who saved me hours of driving through unmarked lanes; and the guides at St Kevin's at Glendalough and St Mary's collegiate church in Gowran in Ireland, whose information and suggestions proved invaluable. Finally, I would like to thank my wife Blanca, who unfailingly manages to spot unnecessary verbiage in my drafts, and whose cheerful encouragement has made it possible for me to undertake this personal little journey around the churches I love.

Benholm Old Kirk

Southwest England

From honey-coloured Cotswold stone to the granite of Cornwall, this region is as rich in its variety and style of churches as it is in its landscapes. Distinctive square West Country church towers with decorated pinnacles at each corner; sturdy Cornish churches of tough granite and slate; the red sandstone of Devon; the chalk and flint of Wiltshire; the bleakness of Dartmoor – all offer unparalleled settings for this wide range of churches.

Restoration at its very best can be seen at All Saints' in North Cerney, an extraordinary 20th-century collaboration between a churchwarden and an architect, while nearby, at St John the Evangelist in Elkstone, Norman stone carving is the overriding glory. Persecution features in this region too – the Loughwood Meeting House at Dalwood is testament to the determination of a congregation to worship freely.

Accidental bomb damage paved the way for outstanding church art in the form of Whistler's etched glass windows at St Nicholas's in Moreton, Dorset, and, at the other end of the timescale and the other side of the region, the Anglo Saxon carvings at St Mary's Church in Deerhurst are a reminder that church ornamentation and art are timeless. And in terms of stone carving, what more human touch could there be than the agonising depiction of a man with toothache on the outside wall of St Mary's Church in Loders.

Perhaps most emblematic of all is St Enodoc at Trebetherick, the medieval church in the middle of a Cornish golf course, and burial place of Sir John Betjeman; it is a fitting resting place for a man whose boundless affection for the English parish church was only matched by his deep devotion.

List of Churches

Abbotsbury, St Nicholas
Alton Priors, All Saints
Atherington, St Mary
Avening, Holy Cross
Beverston, St Mary
Blagdon, St Andrew
Bodmin, St Petroc
Brentor, St Michael de la Rupe
Carhampton, St John the Baptist
Compton Martin, St Michael
    the Archangel
Dalwood, Loughwood Meeting House
Deerhurst, Odda's Chapel
Deerhurst, St Mary
Dolton, St Edmund
Duntisbourne Rouse, St Michael
East Budleigh, Salem Chapel
Elkstone, St John the Evangelist
Fleet, Holy Trinity

Fleet, The Old Church
Idsworth, St Hubert
Inglesham, St John the Baptist
Kempley, St Mary
Loders, St Mary Magdalene
Malmesbury, Malmesbury Abbey
Moreton, St Nicholas
North Cerney, All Saints
Rodhuish, St Bartholomew
Sampford Courtenay, St Andrew
St Columb Major, St Columba
St Ervan Churchtown, St Ervan
St Mawgan-in-Pydar, St Mawgan &
    St Nicholas
Stinsford, St Michael
Trebetherick, St Enodoc
Wareham, Lady St Mary
Wareham, St Martin
Wootton Rivers, St Andrew

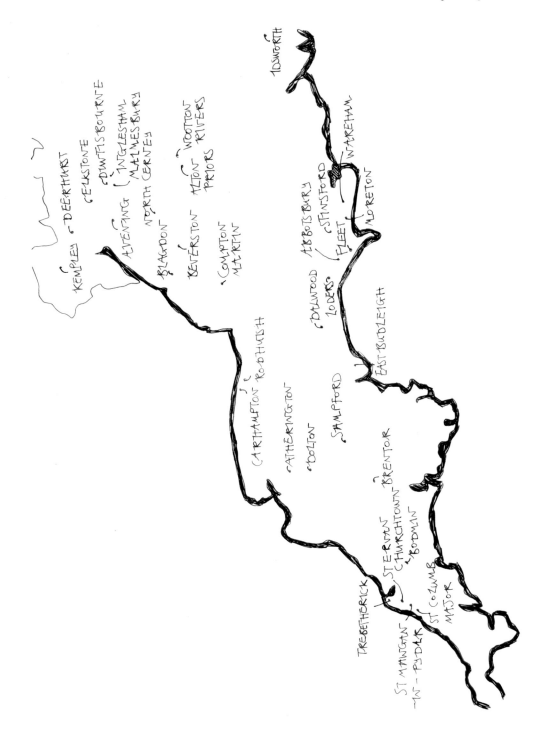

IDSWORTH

WAREHAM

MORETON

FLEET

STINSFORD

ABBOTSBURY

CATISTOCK LODERS

EAST BUDLEIGH

SAMPFORD

BOLTON

CATHERINGTON

CARHAMPTON RODHUISH

COMPTON MARTIN

KEYNSTON MILTON WOOTTON
PRIORS RIVERS

BLAGDON

AVENING INGLESHAM MALMESBURY
NORTH CERNEY

KEMPLEY DEERHURST

ELKSTONE

DUNTISBOURNE

ST ERTH

CHURCHTOWN BRENTOR

BODMIN

TREBETHERICK

ST MINGAN
-IN-PYDAR

ST COLUMB
MAJOR

ABBOTSBURY
St Nicholas

St Nicholas's Church was built by the abbot of the nearby Benedictine monastery but for the use of the parishioners; the monks had their own separate, adjoining church. The dedication to St Nicholas probably owes its origins to the village's seafaring traditions, though some of these were not always approved of: in 1752 a London journal declared that 'All the people of Abbotsbury, including the vicar, are thieves, smugglers, and plunderers of wrecks.'

The Benedictine monastery was founded in the 11th century, but it was not until the late 14th century that the monastery decided to build a separate church, though under the same roof as the monastery church, for parish use. The overall appearance of St Nicholas's is Perpendicular, and it dates from between the 14th and 16th centuries. In the 16th century, the 'double' church was probably unroofed, its south wall demolished, and a new south aisle constructed. Despite its connection to the monastery, the survival of St Nicholas's Church after the dissolution is almost certainly due to its use by the parish.

Inside, the east window of the chancel has been covered by a monolithic mid-18th century wooden reredos displaying the Ten Commandments. The Jacobean pulpit is earlier and it is claimed that two holes in the tester are from bullets during the English Civil War. An interesting late 12th-century stone carving stands in the north porch, showing an abbot, crozier in one hand and book in the other.

Immediately opposite the porch entrance are two 14th-century stone coffins, found underneath the porch when the floor was lowered; above the west door of the tower is inset a stone carving of a seated figure, believed to date from the founding of the monastery.

Nearby: Loders, St Mary Magdalene

ALTON PRIORS
All Saints CCT

This redundant, late medieval church on the edge of a stream looks out at its sister church at Alton Barnes, which is still open for parish use. This is a land of neolithic remains and crop circles, so it comes as no surprise to find out that All Saints' has two megaliths: one is accessible under a

trapdoor on the southeast side of the nave; the other is in the west end.

The church is Norman in origin, although the chancel arch is the only visible sign of this; the rest of the building dates from the 15th and 16th centuries, with a sturdy Perpendicular tower looking out over the surrounding countryside. Inside, limewashed walls and solid rough-cut roof timbers create a pleasant open atmosphere, complemented by a scattering of furnishings, a 16th-century tomb, Jacobean pews, and the communion rails.

ATHERINGTON
St Mary

St Mary's Church is an unmistakable landmark for miles; located on a hilltop in the north Devon village of

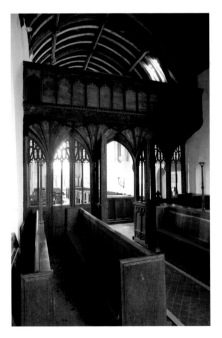

Atherington, it stands high above the surrounding countryside.

The church is noted for possessing the only surviving rood loft in Devon. The loft and the rood screen are in the north aisle, also known as the Bassett aisle. It originally spanned the north aisle and chancel, but, in about 1800, the chancel portion was removed, and replaced with a much inferior chancel screen, thought to have been brought from the nearby demolished Umberleigh Chapel. The original 16th-century rood loft was the work of carvers from Chittlehampton, who probably carved the replacement chancel screen as well. Fine and unusual woodcarving can also be seen in the 15th-century crocketed bench-ends; these include ornaments on pinnacles, and are unusual for the county.

The Bassett family has a conspicuous presence at St Mary's. An altar tomb to Sir John Bassett and his two wives can be found between the chancel and the north aisle, and nearby is a 13th-century effigy of Sir William Champernowne, brought from Umberleigh at the same time as the rood loft. In the chancel are two effigies from the 14th century.

AVENING
Holy Cross

This is a delightful large Cotswold church founded by Queen Matilda, wife of William the Conqueror, and perched at the top of the village of Avening, which lies on the western slope of the Cotswold Hills.

This finely situated church was recorded from 1105 and still retains many Norman features. The oldest parts of the present church, which is built in the form of a cross, date from the late 11th century. A tower was added

in the late 12th century and further additions were made subsequently. A Norman doorway, with twisted columns and dog-tooth moulding, leads through a porch with a parvise above, into the west end of the church which is much as it was when first built. Built into the wall by the door are fragments believed to be from the original Norman font. The church is a very pleasing combination of Norman, Early English and Perpendicular architecture.

An unusual and difficult-to-spot feature of the church is high in the roof beams. It is a carved male exhibitionist figure that crouches under one of the stone corbels.

Nearby: Duntisbourne Rouse, St Michael; Beverston, St Mary

BEVERSTON

St Mary

The salvaged rood screen

St Mary's Church, standing in the shadow of Beverston Castle, was rescued from ruin in 1842. This was not a particularly good restoration; a later restoration in 1884 attempted to remedy the damage. This included reinstating the rood screen, which had been used as a pergola in the rector's garden.

The use of the rood screen as a garden feature was not the only damage. The font had been 'improved' by hacking off the old stone carving, and old wall paintings had been plastered over. One important feature that did survive was a fine – if somewhat damaged – Saxon carving of Christ with his hand raised in blessing. This can be seen on the south face of the tower. In the south aisle, between the

19th-century Gothic windows, is a fine Norman doorway. The roof is strange: it is believed to have been designed by the architect Louis Vulliamy, and is a maze of oddly angled trusses and corbels, a complicated engineering solution for a church of such elegant simplicity.

Nearby: Avening, Holy Cross

BLAGDON
St Andrew

This is an elegant Somerset church whose Perpendicular tower, one of the highest in the county, soars above a surrounding screen of trees.

St Andrew's is a 15th-century church; its nave, chancel and aisles were rebuilt and restored at the beginning of the 20th century, replacing a very poor and unnecessary 19th-century rebuilding. The restoration of St Andrew's to its original Gothic form owes much to two members of the Wills tobacco family, Lord Winterstoke and Sir Frank Wills, architect, one time Lord Mayor of Bristol, and son of Henry Overton Wills.

The church has an airy feel to it, partly because, unusually, it is almost square in plan. Little remains of the earlier church, except for the piscina, which depicts the four Evangelists. Despite the absence of original features and fittings, the spirit and essence of the original church have been recaptured. The arcades and chancel arch have broad and well-proportioned arches. The chancel, in which hangs a striking painting of the Last Supper by Oswald Moser, is divided from the nave by a exceptionally well-carved rood screen and loft; this was added in 1935, and, in common with the rest of the furnishings and fittings, captures the spirit of a much earlier age. At the west end of the north aisle is a memorial window to Augustus Toplady, the composer of 'Rock of Ages', who spent his first curacy at St Andrew's.

Nearby: Compton Martin, St Michael the Archangel

BODMIN
St Petroc

Of the many Cornish saints, St Petroc is perhaps the one closest to the hearts of Cornishmen. Apart from the towns and settlements whose names derive from Petroc, the monasticism he started in Bodmin turned the town into the religious capital of Cornwall until the late Middle Ages.

St Petroc's is the largest parish church in Cornwall, and is 'Cornish Perpendicular' in style. It houses the much-travelled relics of St Petroc, which were originally moved there from Padstow in the hope of preserving them from the marauding Danes in the 10th century. In the 12th century the remains were stolen and taken to the Abbey of St Meen in Brittany, either by a disgruntled canon of Bodmin, or by visiting French monks, who were said to have taunted the Cornish about their belief in King Arthur. The relics were soon returned to Bodmin with 'due honour, apology and homage', and survived the Reformation concealed in the south porch. In 1994 the reliquary was stolen again and was later found in a Yorkshire field. The relics of St Petroc are now in their rightful place again, albeit rather better protected than before.

Nearby: St Columb Major, St Columba

BRENTOR
St Michael de la Rupe

Built in the 12th century, this lonely Dartmoor church stands on a volcanic outcrop on the brink of a precipice. On the eastern slopes of the tor are the remains of an Iron Age fort. In addition to being the highest parish church in England, St Michael's is also the fourth-smallest; it is built from volcanic rock taken from its rocky perch.

The church dates from around the 13th century, although records refer to a church here in the mid-10th century. St Michael's has few particular distinguishing architectural details, apart from the thickness of the base of the walls – these are about ten feet thick. The tower may date from the 15th century, and is pierced with drainage holes to deal with the water that seeps in through the porous granite. The louvred bell chamber openings have been fitted with movable shutters to keep out the driving Dartmoor rains.

CARHAMPTON
St John the Baptist

The church of St John the Baptist is in a small village on a busy road between Williton and Minehead, a place that is driven through rather than visited. The church is easily missed, but contains a superb eleven-bay rood screen. An ancient carters' right of way runs through the churchyard, which also has a mounting block by the main gate.

St John the Baptist's is a 15th-century church, Perpendicular in style; it was completely restored between 1862 and 1864, with a nave and south aisle. The north wall and tower were rebuilt in typical Somerset style, with stair turret and crocketed finials. Most of the original features were retained: the original barrel-vaulted roof, carved bosses, and an attractive 18th-century pulpit.

The very fine Perpendicular rood screen was also kept. Despite the absence of the rood loft, this screen is an outstanding piece of furnishing: its bays of finely carved Perpendicular tracery, separated by fine fan vaulting, support an intricately ornamented panel that spans the entire width of the nave and south aisle. The screen is richly painted and gilded, work done by the Victorian restorers. It is not known whether there were remnants of the original paint to guide them, but the work is certainly in the spirit of early medieval rood screen decoration; it is a bold and interesting piece of restoration.

Nearby: Rodhuish, St Bartholomew

county, in which the officials had no jurisdiction; members of the congregation would take it in turns to keep watch during a meeting. Curiously, Baptist zeal actually declined following the 1689 Act of Toleration.

During the early years the chapel was an austere sombre place; the one concession to comfort was a fire, much needed for those who had been immersed in the spring-fed baptistry under the floor. In the early 18th century the chapel acquired some more comfort in the form of box pews and a west gallery.

DEERHURST
Odda's Chapel

It was only in the latter part of the 19th century that the significance of this remote Saxon chapel on the banks of the River Severn came to light; until then it had been incorporated into the adjoining Tudor farmhouse.

Despite being next to one of the most interesting Anglo Saxon churches in England – St Mary's priory church – Odda's Chapel should not be overlooked. This chapel is a simple nave and chancel church, founded by Earl Odda, one of the most influential Saxon nobles during Edward the Confessor's reign. It is a simple two-cell church, completed about the year 1056. Inside, the chapel is bare and plain, but the chancel arch remains, as do the original windows. Typical Saxon stonework can be seen in the use of long and short quoins. The original dedication stone is now in the Ashmolean Museum in Oxford, but a reproduction in the chapel reads, 'EARL ODDA HAD THIS ROYAL HALL BUILT AND DEDICATED IN HONOUR OF THE HOLY TRINITY FOR THE SOUL OF HIS BROTHER, AELFRIC, WHICH LEFT THE BODY IN THIS PLACE. BISHOP EAL- DRED DEDICATED IT THE SECOND OF THE IDES OF APRIL IN THE FOURTEENTH YEAR OF THE REIGN OF EDWARD, KING OF THE ENGLISH.'

Nearby: Deerhurst, St Mary

DEERHURST
St Mary

This Anglo Saxon church continues to surprise with evidence of its Saxon past; a recent discovery revealed the existence of a painted figure of a saint holding a book on a stone panel high up in the east nave wall; it is thought to date from the 10th century.

From a distance, though, St Mary's hides its Anglo Saxon origins well. The adjoining farmhouse (once part of the priory buildings), the clerestory above the nave, the Tudor south aisle and the tower all give the impression of a medieval building. But all this is deceptive. Above the hood-moulding over the west door and thought to be from the 9th century, a carved stone beast rears from the masonry. Through the porch, above the inner doorway, is an early carving of the Virgin and Child, still with traces of the original colouring, thought to have been

moved to its present position from the ruined apse. In the northeast corner is a splendid carved 9th-century font with 'Celtic trumpet spirals'. Herringbone masonry has been uncovered in the northeast corner, where one can also see traces of doorways that led to Saxon side chapels. Two carved wolf heads – originally terminations of the outside hood-moulding – now flank the west end archway, while, high on the west wall of the high narrow nave, are slab-headed Saxon windows, opening into a now inaccessible chapel. Outside, at the east end of the church, are the foundations and blocked archway of

the original polygonal apse, and, high on the exterior of the surviving southern section of the apse walls, is a stone panel with a carved angel.

Later ages have added considerable interest too. There are 13th-century Early English arcades. The west window in the south aisle has glass showing St Catherine and the famous wheel. In the northeast corner a 14th century brass to the Cassey family set in the floor depicts the family pet, a dog named Terri. This is possibly the first memorial of its kind on which a named pet is depicted.

Nearby: Deerhurst, Odda's Chapel

DOLTON
St Edmund

The declared aim of the Victorian restoration of St Edmund's Church was to have 'no pretensions to beauty of architecture or style', an aim that the builders achieved internally in some style. The medieval character of St Edmund's, in a remote and little-visited Devon village, was almost completely lost as a consequence of this 'hard' restoration, although, from the outside, the church has a very pleasing appearance. Among the few surviving features are four 16th-century bench-ends, and, at the west end of the nave, a memorial to a 17th-century rector, William Knaplock.

But there is an outstanding surprise inside the church: an important Anglo Saxon font. It is unique, in that it is formed of two carved stone blocks that may originally have come from either one or two stone cross-shafts. The upper block is inverted, and was hollowed out from its base. Three of its four sides are carved with a Scandinavian-style serpentine motif, entwined around a human face, dragon-like creatures and fish. The lower section has intricate and finely carved interlaced patterns. This font is thought to be at least a thousand years old, and its origins are still the subject of debate.

DUNTISBOURNE ROUSE
St Michael

St Michael's Chapel is cut into the side of a quiet Cotswold valley, overlooking the River Dunt. Its chancel has the remains of early Norman wall paintings, including one of a monk with a harp, first uncovered in 1872 by the Revd George Moberly, whose original notes about the paintings sadly have gaps in them caused by church mice.

The sloping site of St Michael's Chapel allowed the builders to place the chancel over a crypt. The building

is late Saxon or early Norman; one theory is that the first church was the nave, and that the Norman builders added the chancel and crypt. A commentator at the beginning of the 1800s censoriously suggests that the crypt was used for 'some superstitious purposes of the Romish worship', and it is not unreasonable to assume that there may have been a relic in the crypt, with the faithful approaching down the steps from the chancel and exiting through the lower door.

Nearby: Avening, Holy Cross; Elkstone, St John the Evangelist; North Cerney, All Saints

EAST BUDLEIGH
Salem Chapel HCT

This square cob-and-stone Presbyterian chapel on the edge of the village was presumably named for the founder of Salem, Massachusetts, Roger Conant, who was born in East Budleigh. In the grounds are a small graveyard and schoolroom.

The inside of this tiny chapel is lined on three sides with panelled galleries supported on slender cast-iron posts. The fine vaulted ceiling has a good moulded and bracketed cornice, and, like the galleries, was originally supported by an iron post. No village whose sons have been eminent seafarers could possibly do without its tales of smuggling, and so it is here, where Samuel Leat, minister in the latter part of the 18th century, made himself wealthy through the proceeds of smuggling. He also extended his monetary improvisation to the embezzlement of chapel funds, and his coffin is said to have been disinterred and desecrated.

ELKSTONE
St John the Evangelist

An entertaining parade of heads looks down from the corbel table that runs along the nave wall at St John's Church, which shelters behind a screen of pine trees in this exposed and wind-scoured part of the Cotswolds.

From the outside, the outline of the church shows that the chancel stands higher than the nave: there is a columbarium in the roof space above, reached from a small stairway behind the pulpit. Above the south door is a superb tympanum, carved in reverse relief. It shows Christ seated: in his left hand he holds the Book of Judgement, with his right hand raised in benediction. Surrounding the scene is a succession of beak-head ornaments, and, in the outermost order, excellent chevron decoration.

Not even this Norman entrance can prepare one for the inside, however: once through the door, and to the east, a beautifully patterned chancel arch terminates in two ferocious wolf heads and leads to a short stone-vaulted choir area. Another finely decorated lower arch leads to the sanctuary; at the east end over the altar is a window with elaborately carved surrounds. There is a wonderful effect of light and colour from the stained glass at the east end of the chancel, and more particularly the golden light from the modern glass in the south chancel windows, the work of WT Carter Shapland.

Nearby: Duntisbourne Rouse, St Michael; North Cerney, All Saints

St Hubert

Locals know St Hubert's Chapel as 'The Little Church in the Field'; at the top of a rise in the soft downland contours, it is a familiar sight to commuters on passing trains.

There was a village here, and a local manor too: the village existed between the 9th and 14th centuries and the manor was demolished in the 19th century with the advent of the railway line. The chapel is kept bright and clean by parishioners, and services are regularly held.

The chapel was originally dedicated to St Peter: it was only after the discovery of the wall painting on the north chancel wall in 1864 that it was rededicated to St Hubert, patron saint of hunters. The painting is thought to date from around 1330 and was originally believed to depict St Hubert converting a lycanthrope. A more contemporary interpretation is that the scene is more likely to be a depiction of the discovery of a 'hairy anchorite', a hermit who undertook a penance of walking on all fours. On the right-hand side can be seen the arrest of St John the Baptist; to the left St John being imprisoned; and the lower right part depicts his head on a salver.

INGLESHAM
St John the Baptist

St John's Church stands on a slight rise, elevated from the surrounding water meadows and the nearby River Thames. It has a fine collection of wall paintings and a Saxon carving of the Mother and Child set in the wall.

St John's Church is like a time capsule: it has wall paintings from several centuries; a 14th-century door; a font from the 15th century; pews and screens from the 16th century; a 17th-century pulpit, and communion rails from the 18th century. William Morris and the Society for the Protection of Ancient Buildings took on the task of preserving this church from the over-zealous attention of the Cambridge Camden Society of ecclesiologists, to whom non-Gothic was anathema.

The wall paintings are the most interesting, being almost graffiti-like; the walls appear to have been seen as a surface on which anyone could paint.

In places, the wall paintings are seven layers thick: 19th-century texts, 15th-century angels and a 14th-century Doom all jostle with each other. It is a mixture that we might deplore if it came from our own time, but, in the context of St John's church, it has a historical fascination.

KEMPLEY
St Mary

There are two churches in Kempley, a small village set in the rural landscape of north Gloucestershire. The relatively modern Arts and Crafts church

and, on the west wall, an explosion of swirling light known as the Galaxy Window. Even the porch has beautiful, simply designed memorial windows by Whistler. Though these windows were not originally popular with parishioners, the work is of astonishing quality, with a profound spiritual dimension, and, frankly, eclipses everything else within the church.

Those who come to visit the grave of T E Lawrence (Lawrence of Arabia) in the cemetery should make sure to come to this exquisite church too.

Nearby: Stinsford, St Michael

NORTH CERNEY
All Saints

All Saints' is set in the picturesque Churn valley. It is a church of great charm, whose churchyard is kept in order by grazing sheep, and owes its appearance to both the 15th and 20th centuries.

In the mid 1400s, a fire destroyed most of the 12th- and 13th-century building, the saddleback tower acting like a furnace chimney. The subsequent restoration was financed from local wool wealth.

Its present day medieval interior, however, is mainly the result of a fine collaboration between the churchwarden William Iveson Croome, and

the architect Frederick c Eden, whose restoration took place in the first part of the 20th century. Their imagination and creativity brought together fine craftsmanship and a host of authentic treasures. The rood loft was carved locally to Eden's design, as were the figures flanking the 1600s Crucifixion, found in an Italian antique shop by William Croome. The High Altar frontal comes from a remnant of material woven for Chartres Cathedral; the reredos is the work of Eden, as is the south transept screen. Altars were reinstated in the chapels, and, in the Lady Chapel, three 15th-century

statues of St Martin, St Urban and the Virgin, look tailor-made for their setting above the altar. The 16th-century lectern top in Flemish brass was found in a Gloucester chandler's store, and the reading desk was made from an old box pew.

This was an exemplary restoration, harmoniously conceived, and executed with knowledgeable flair and a gift for improvisation.

Nearby: Duntisbourne Rouse, St Michael; Elkstone, St John the Evangelist

RODHUISH
St Bartholomew

St Bartholomew's Chapel is remote, set in farmland at the edge of the Exmoor National Park and surrounded by wild meadow flowers and grasses. It is a church of charming simplicity and is held in great affection by its congregation. With support from its parishioners, English Heritage, and the Golsoncott Foundation, the chapel has recently been fully restored.

St Bartholomew's is a low, croftlike building dating from the 13th century, with an enclosed belfry at the west end. Inside, a plain Norman font from

nearby Carhampton stands underneath the west gallery. The nave and chancel are lit by windows with simple Geometric tracery, and over the whole chapel is a fine wooden wagon-roof. An interesting sculpture of Jacob wrestling with the Angel stands in the south corner of the chancel; this is the work of master wood engraver turned metal sculptor Rachel Reckitt.

There is no electricity in this peaceful little place, just the delight of candlelit services and music recitals.

Nearby: Carhampton, St John the Baptist

ST COLUMB MAJOR
St Columba

This imposing church stands at the head of the Vale of Lanherne, and in the 19th century, despite the best efforts of wealthy incumbent Dr Walker, narrowly lost out to Truro as the cathedral church of Cornwall.

A medieval college stood adjacent

to the church, provided by Sir John Arundel for six priests whose duties were to pray for departed family members in the newly constructed chantry chapel of Our Lady; the college was destroyed by accidental fire in 1701. The Perpendicular tower is unusual, in that a 'through-passage' runs from north to south at its base. This passageway was broad enough to admit the passage of a cart, and may have provided parishioners with a right of way to the medieval college. Looked at from the east, the body of the church is formed of three main parts: the nave, and two flanking broad aisles. The east end of the north aisle and nave have fine Perpendicular windows, while that of the south aisle is Geometric–Curvilinear.

The rood screen has an interesting history: the original Tudor screen was removed by a rector in the late 19th century, much to the disapproval of his son, whose first act upon succeeding his father as rector was to reinstate the screen. Other wood carving fared better: throughout the church there are some fine early carved bench-ends, including one of a bear dancing to music provided by a monkey.

Nearby: St Ervan Churchtown, St Ervan; St Mawgan-in-Pydar, St Mawgan and St Nicholas

ST ERVAN CHURCHTOWN
St Ervan

This is the church mentioned by John Betjeman in his poem 'Summoned by Bells'. It is easy to sense the charm that this delightful church must have exerted over the poet. It is almost untouched: 13th and 14th century; cruciform, with an odd kink in the alignment of the chancel; it is reached by a narrow tree-lined lane. When Betjeman first came across the church, cycling through narrow Cornish lanes, the bell would have been suspended from a wooden frame outside the porch.

In contrast to the generally good condition of this parish church, however, the tower has suffered badly. The original tower was built some time between the 14th and 15th centuries, had two stages and an embattled roof. In the 19th century it became unsafe, and, despite attempted repairs, continued to show signs of instability. The parishioners, anticipating a possible collapse, attempted and failed to pull it down using a team of horses, and then resorted to dynamiting the upper stage of the tower. Other than temporary repairs, nothing was then done until the 1950s, when the tower was partially reconstructed with concrete blocks and rendering, and topped with a pyramidal roof. Now

St Ervan's has a 24-foot tower rather than a 50-foot one.

A charming carved wooden angel (left) affixed to the south door welcomes one into a simple nave and transept building, with Perpendicular windows and a chancel that has a distinct kink to the right. On the walls are a number of interesting memorials, including an incised slate with a macabre skull at the bottom. Sadly, the Victorian restoration removed all the Georgian box pews, the pulpit and the west gallery; the pulpit, however, was later discovered in the rectory garden, and reinstated in the church. But St Ervan's has transcended the Victorian zeal, keeping a sense of peaceful detachment from the things of the world.

Nearby: St Columb Major, St Columba; St Mawgan-in-Pydar, St Mawgan and St Nicholas

ST MAWGAN-IN-PYDAR
St Mawgan and St Nicholas

The setting of St Mawgan's is quintessentially English: old cottages and a village lie to the east; the River Menalhyl runs cheerfully under a stone bridge to the north; and the church is framed by a wooded slope.

Just inside the lych gate is the ancient well of St Mawgan, and close by is a granite Hurling Trough. Up the path and past the tower is the upper churchyard, where there is a most unusual and intricately carved stone

15th-century lantern cross; it is extremely weathered, but it is still possible to discern detail. Above, shaded by trees is a melancholy maritime memorial, the inscribed transom of a rowing boat. It marks the burial place of ten people 'who were drifted ashore, frozen to death at Tregurrian Beach in this parish'.

The staunch Loyalist Arundell family are commemorated in the Lady Chapel by two fine 16th-century brasses, and the church still displays Charles I's Letter of Thanks, written to all loyal churches in Cornwall.

Nearby: St Columb Major, St Columba; St Ervan Churchtown, St Ervan

SAMPFORD COURTENAY
St Andrew

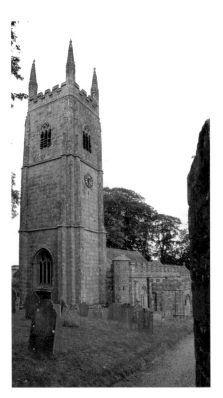

The gracious Perpendicular outlines of St Andrew's give no hint of the violent rebellion that was sparked in this 16th-century stronghold of traditional Catholicism. Whitsunday 1549 marked the beginning of the Prayer Book Rebellion: the congregation at St Andrew's flew in the face of Edward VI's edict that enforced the use of the English prayer book, and forced the parish priest to celebrate the old Latin mass. The parishioners protested that the English liturgy was 'but lyke a Christmas game'. Magistrates were called to a subsequent service, and, during an argument, William Hellyons, a supporter of the edict, was killed with a pitchfork. The ensuing rebellion was brutally suppressed after the failed siege of Exeter.

The church was rebuilt during the

Wars of the Roses in the late 15th century, and is spacious and light. A broad nave opens on to the north and south aisles. The pillars of the north arcade are of granite, and those on the south are of Cornish polyphant stone, much softer and easier to carve. Interesting carved wooden roof bosses can be seen around the church. A serene head stands above the altar, and close by is a green man. The church lost its rood screen in the 19th century at the direction of the incumbent rector; fortunately a sufficiently large part was recovered to reinstate the south chancel portion of the screen.

STINSFORD
St Michael

This is a Thomas Hardy church – the Mellstock of his novels and poems – and his heart is buried in the church-yard. Another great poet is buried here too – Cecil Day-Lewis, Poet Laureate from 1967 to 1972; as a great admirer of Hardy, he wanted to be buried as close to him as possible.

The Hardy family had a long associ-ation with St Michael's Church – Hardy's father was a keen member of the church band, in which he played the bass viol – and the burial of Hardy's heart at Stinsford was a com-promise. While his heart was buried next to the grave of his first wife, Hardy's ashes were interred in Westminster Abbey.

St Michael's is a typical small English village church, Norman in origin, with modest Perpendicular additions. The atmosphere inside is comfortably rustic, especially around harvest time, when the church is decked out with sheaves of corn and barley. A new west gallery, rededicated

in 1996, fills the space left when the old gallery in which the Hardys played the bass viol and fiddle. It also contains the organ, a change in position that Thomas Hardy once recommended.

Nearby: Moreton, St Nicholas

TREBETHERICK
St Enodoc

St Enodoc's church sits in the middle of the fairways of the local golf club, surrounded by sand dunes at the edge of Daymer Bay. The poet John Betjeman is buried just inside the lych gate, to the right, and the church is celebrated in Betjeman's poem 'Sunday Afternoon Service in St Enodoc Church, Cornwall'.

St Enodoc's can only be reached on foot, and one's first sight of this little 15th-century chapel of ease is of a short, crooked octagonal stone spire, its top covered in lichen, peering over a high hedge. The hedge shelters St Enodoc's church from the winds that come in from the sea, and the sand that comes with it; the best viewpoint is from nearby Brea Hill.

St Enodoc's dates from the 12th century, although most of what exists now is from the 15th century. It is a small church with nave and chancel, it has a north transept joined to the tower, and a short south transept. In the 18th and 19th centuries the church was neglected and almost became lost in the sands; the only access was through a purpose-built skylight. Before a radical restoration under-taken by the vicar in the mid 1800s, his son wrote an account of the state of the church, in which he commented that, 'the sands had blown higher than the eastern gable, the wet came in freely, the high pews were mouldy-green and worm-eaten and bats flew about, living in the belfry. The communion table had two short legs to allow for the rock projecting at the foot of the east wall.'

WAREHAM
Lady St Mary

The tower of this Wareham church is a landmark for vessels sailing up the River Frome from Poole, and stands behind the former priory buildings, which are now a hotel.

In 1840 it was reported that the roof was dilapidated, and complaints were frequently made that the nave was too dark. A scheme of rebuilding was undertaken that illustrates the worst aspect of Victorian church 'restoration'. If the roof was going to be renewed, then why not rebuild the nave at the same time? Demolition in 1841 was by dynamite – a staggering and controversial act of vandalism in a church that is thought to be one of the earliest of the larger Saxon churches. Ironically, the demolition exposed a series of very interesting early Celtic memorial stones, some of which date from the 7th century; these can be seen in the north aisle, and suggest that there may have been an even earlier Celtic church on the site.

Thankfully, many other outstanding features of Lady St Mary remain unchanged. On the south side of the chancel are a double piscina and a staggered three-part sedilia, and to the south of the chancel is one of the church's unexpected treasures, St Edward's Chapel. A 14th-century tomb recess arch, taken from elsewhere in the church, leads to a Norman archway which in turn opens into a small, rib-vaulted chapel, with 13th-century tomb recesses set left

and right. This chapel is a simple and quiet space, dedicated to Edward, King and Martyr, murdered at Corfe Castle, and buried at Wareham briefly, before being moved to Shaftesbury.

At the other end of the church is an outstanding 12th-century cast-lead font, one of only 30 in the country, and unique for its hexagonal shape. A continuous arcade encloses figures of the Twelve Apostles, and the basin is set on Purbeck marble. And in the west walls of both aisles there are still traces of Saxon Stonework.

Nearby: Wareham, St Martin

WAREHAM
St Martin

St Martin's Church is one of the few buildings that survived Wareham's Great Fire in 1762. It is built on the north town wall on a site thought to have been occupied by a Roman temple.

St Martin's is one of the few late

Saxon churches in Dorset to retain its original form. Built around 1030, it has the typical narrow high nave of a Saxon building. On the north chancel wall are painted scenes depicting the story of how St Martin shared his cloak with a beggar. Although the paintings have faded, it is still possible to make out a considerable amount of detail.

In the north aisle is a fine sculpted effigy of TE Lawrence, showing him in traditional Arab robes, with his feet against two fighting dogs. The memorial was never intended for St Martin's: its proposed home was St Paul's Cathedral in London, but, as there was some controversy surrounding Lawrence's involvement with the Arabs during the war, St Paul's decided not to take it. A similar response came from Westminster Abbey, and from Salisbury Cathedral; the effigy found its final place in the modest but venerable surroundings of St Martin's.

Nearby: Wareham, Lady St Mary

WOOTTON RIVERS
St Andrew

Although Saxon origins are claimed for this modest little church, its present-day appearance is mostly due to a Victorian restoration in the mid-19th century, although its fame lies in the entertaining story of the clock that can be found there.

In 1911 cities, towns and villages throughout England were finding different ways to mark the coronation of George V. The incumbent of Wootton, the Revd Alcock suggested that a public coronation clock should be made and installed in the church. The purses of the village ran mysteriously dry at this suggestion, and a counter-proposal of a celebration dinner was adopted.

One villager decided to pursue the idea of the clock, however: John Kingstone Spratt, a former farm labourer turned 'clock man', offered to make a clock, provided that the village would supply him with scrap brass, lead, steel and iron. Amid much derision, he succeeded – with the help of neighbouring craftsmen – in making a three-faced clock, which was kept going by two large hand-wound lead weights, and whose chimes are run by a musical box arrangement of studs on a rotating drum that trigger hammers for particular bells. Made from bits of ploughshare, brass bedsteads and broom handles, the clock still works, although repairs by professional clockmakers are gradually changing the Heath Robinson character of the original clock.

London and the South East

It is still possible to find surprisingly quiet and lonely corners in this densely populated corner of England. Outstanding old churches can be found throughout Kent, some of them in deep isolation. Bonnington's St Rumwold's claims to be the oldest church on Romney Marsh, while the church of St Thomas à Becket in Fairfield sits timelessly amid dykes and rough marsh pasture. The north of the county is a swirl of traffic, commuters, riverside industry and people in transit, yet St James in Cooling, within sight of oil refineries, manages to convey a sense of detachment from the bustle of 21st-century life.

To the west of the region, the landscape takes on a different look – chalk downland and beech woods. St Mary's in Stoughton is an excellent example of a Saxon church, while St Michael's in nearby Up Marden is a country church at its most rudimentary, and steeped in rural atmosphere. All Saints' in Minstead, on the edge of the New Forest, couldn't be more different. This is a 'country house' church, all gabled windows and random extensions.

Boxgrove Priory church exemplifies the monastic – a fine combination of Norman and Early English architecture, while the little Church of St Botolph in Hardham is filled with early 12th-century wall paintings.

Not all are old: one of the great treasures of the region is from the 20th century: the magnificent Marc Chagall stained-glass windows at All Saints' in Tudeley, memorials of a tragic sailing accident.

List of Churches

Albury, St Peter & St Paul
Barfreston, St Nicholas
Bonnington, St Rumwold
Bosham, Holy Trinity
Botolphs, St Botolph
Boxgrove, St Mary & St Blaise
Brookland, St Augustine
Church Norton, St Wilfrid
Compton, Watts Cemetery Chapel
Cooling, St James
Didling, St Andrew
Esher, St George
Etchingham, The Assumption of
    Blessed Mary & St Nicholas
Fairfield, St Thomas à Becket
Hardham, St Botolph
London – Clerkenwell, St Peter
London – Fleet Street,
    St Dunstan-in-the-West

London – Hampstead, St John at
    Hampstead
London – Leicester Place, Notre Dame
    de France
London – Pimlico, St Barnabas
Lower Higham, St Mary
Minstead, All Saints
New Romney, St Nicholas
Old Romney, St Clement
Romsey, St Mary & St Aethelflaeda
Ruckinge, St Mary Magdalene
Singleton, The Blessed Virgin Mary
South Harting, St Mary & St Gabriel
Stoughton, St Mary
Tudeley, All Saints
Up Marden, St Michael

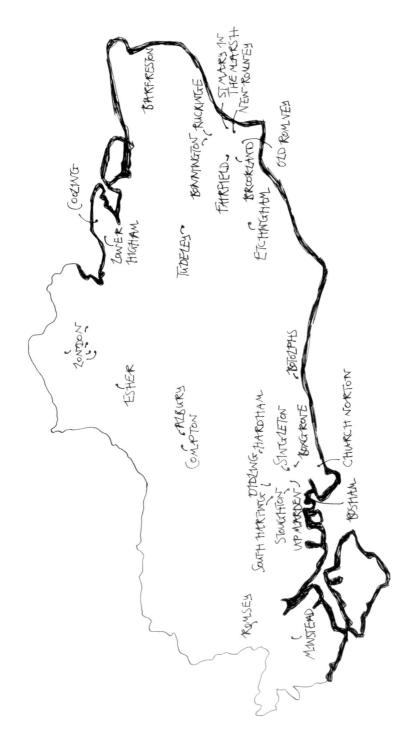

ALBURY
St Peter and St Paul CCT

The Church of St Peter and St Paul stands in the parkland of Albury Park. A building that pre-dates the Norman Conquest, its south chapel is a tribute to the work of the eminent Victorian Gothic revivalist Augustus Pugin.

St Peter and St Paul's Church was once at the centre of a thriving village, but now stands alone in a tranquil setting in the middle of Albury Park. The church is surrounded by trees, close to the River Tilling and, in the late winter, the churchyard is a sea of snowdrops.

Seen from outside, two features are prominent. One is the unusual 18th-century cupola set on the tower; the other is the disproportionately large, Gothic tracery window in the south wall of the south transept. This is the memorial chapel created by architect and designer Augustus Pugin for the Drummond family, who occupied Albury Park. It is a splendid ornate expression of Gothic revival, with painted walls and ceilings and a fine tiled floor, all illuminated by the stained glass in the south window.

BARFRESTON
St Nicholas

This tiny Norman church in Kent is southeast England's equivalent to Herefordshire's St Mary and St David in Kilpeck, although in a less romantic setting. As in Kilpeck the quality and variety of the Romanesque stone carving at St Nicholas's is outstanding.

These extraordinary carvings date from the late 12th century and are a valedictory statement of Norman carving before the advent of French Gothic. St Nicholas's church is a building where the decorative elements are in harmony. The lower courses of the building are flint rubble, and the upper walls are of dressed Caen stone. A continuous string-course runs around the entire church, as does the corbel table above, and the two enclose an arcade that is part blind, part fenestrated. The south doorway supports a superb tympanum, rich in subject matter and quality of carving.

Less often mentioned is the wheel window at the east end of the chancel; these are usually found on churches of larger scale. The window is surrounded by a frieze of intricate detail: a parade of griffins, winged angels and other beasts interspersed

with foliate motifs; the radiating spokes, columnar in form, terminate in capitals carved with staring faces. Every part of the window, as with the carvings elsewhere, shows the same attention to detail.

The inside of the church is simple, but also of interest: intricately carved string-courses run round both the nave and chancel. The finely carved chancel arch stands on barley twist columns and is flanked by two equally fine blind arches with chevron patterning, intended to contain side altars.

BONNINGTON
St Rumwold

St Rumwold's claims to be the oldest church on Romney Marsh, competing for that position with St Nicholas's in New Romney. It is profoundly rural, has no electricity, and stands close by the Royal Military Canal.

This is one of the most tranquil settings imaginable: on a summer day you can hear the skylarks and the rustling of grass and reeds in the wind. Its claims of Saxon origin are based on the relative size of the

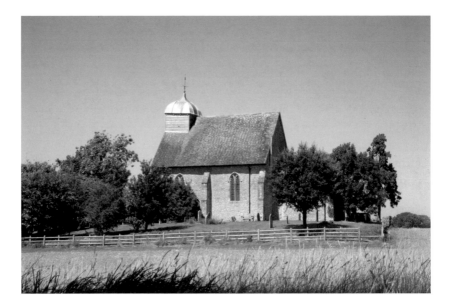

chancel and nave, and the presence of long and short quoining in the south-east corner.

Whether or not it is the oldest marsh church, however, it certainly has indications of early Norman origin. In the east wall of the chancel are three small and deeply splayed Norman windows. There is an interesting double piscina set in the east wall, illustrating a short-lived custom of having one basin for the ceremonial washing of hands, and another for the rinsing out of the chalice. This feature eventually became redundant as the priest was required to drink the water used to rinse the chalice.

The 14th-century windows, mostly with clear glass, admit a pleasant amount of light into the nave, and, in the northwest window, are set some interesting fragments of old stained glass that include a fine half-figure representation of Christ. A Georgian pulpit and tester is set to the south of the chancel arch, while at the west end of the nave is a Jacobean gallery of domineering presence and unusual configuration. Oak timber supports to either side are set free of the nave floor, and the gallery is positioned high up in the gable, from where the view of the chancel is oddly obstructed by the tie beam and king post at the centre of the nave.

BOSHAM
Holy Trinity

The tower and spire of Holy Trinity Church form an unmistakable landmark on a little peninsula between two tidal creeks at the eastern end of Chichester's inland harbour.

This is a fine example of a church with Saxon origins. King Harold II – best known for the Battle of Hastings – visited the church and the visit is depicted in the Bayeux Tapestry; King Cnut's daughter, thought to have drowned nearby, is buried by the chancel arch. The church embraces three main architectural styles – Saxon, Norman and Early English – and the Fishbourne Chantry has Perpendicular windows. The crypt is believed to date from the 14th century, as does the south aisle.

Such is the magnificence of some of the features of the church – the outstanding Early English chancel arch, for example – and so powerful the overall impression of the Saxon

Carving on pediment in the north aisle

church, that the minor details can be easily overlooked. The north aisle contains a recessed piscina drained by a hollow supporting column; tiny fragments of carved Saxon stone set in the wall of the north aisle may have come from a Saxon screen; outside, remains of a very early corbel table can be seen under the eaves of the spire; herringbone masonry characteristic of early Norman masonry techniques can be seen in the south wall of the chancel. Easily missed because of its position is the pier of one column in the north aisle arcade – it has four extraordinary fanged heads carved at each corner of what appears to be a single serpentine body encircling the column. It is an ingenious design, probably early Norman.

Nearby: Singleton, The Blessed Virgin Mary; Stoughton, St Mary; Up Marden, St Michael

BOTOLPHS
St Botolph

St Botolph's is something of a church 'lost and found'. It is situated in the Adur Valley, and is the parish church of one of West Sussex's smallest villages. In fact the village had all but disappeared by the 16th century, and

mounds marking the sites of former dwellings can be seen around the site. This downturn in the local population made St Botolph's one of the earliest churches to suffer redundancy.

The church is Anglo Saxon in

origin, built of flint rubble in 950 AD, and consists of a long, narrow nave with a small square chancel and west tower, both of which date from the 12th century. The chancel arch is certainly pre-Norman, and around it are traces of wall painting, recorded at the end of the 19th century though unfortunately too scant to allow for restoration, but one can still make out the figure of an abbot. In the chancel there are two low-level squint windows, possibly placed there to allow lepers from the Bramber's Hospital of St Mary Magdalene to follow the celebration of mass.

In the mid-14th century the sea began to recede and the village's fortunes went into dramatic decline; by 1534 the parish of Botolphs was united with that of Bramber. The building deteriorated over the centuries and, in the early 19th century, the 13th-century north aisle was demolished, leaving only the filled-in, three-bay arcade to indicate its former presence.

St Botolph's Church is a small but appealing glimpse of the past in this corner of West Sussex, where it offers a series of services associated with the yearly cycle of farming – a refreshing counterbalance to the traffic speeding by on a major road half a mile north.

BOXGROVE
St Mary and St Blaise

Boxgrove Priory was a Benedictine monastery founded by monks from Lessay in Normandy. Since the dissolution, the priory church, set in the ruins of the former priory's domestic buildings, has served as the Parish Church of St Mary and St Blaise.

There were originally two churches here: the monastic church occupied the choir and chancel east of the crossing; a separate parish area was in the now-ruined nave, west of the

Far left: Arts and Crafts stained glass in the south aisle.
Left: Rib-vaulted 16th century nave ceiling

crossing. A stone screen now closes off the crossing from the site of the old nave, but traces of a doorway still remain.

Considering the size of the present nave and chancel – the entire area to the east of the transepts – this was, by any standards, a vast priory church. The prevalent styles are a mixture of 12th-century Norman – predominant at the west end – and 13th-century Early English – seen at its best in the marble- and stone-pillared arcades separating the choir from the aisles. At the east end of the nave is a sanctuary area with a carved reredos by Sir George Gilbert Scott, set above which are three lofty and elegantly proportioned lancet windows, each now filled with Victorian stained glass. And over the nave is the rib-vaulted 16th-century painted ceiling by artist Lambert Barnard, with fine floral patterning and heraldry.

Adjoining the south aisle is the Gothic chantry chapel of the de la Warr family, sumptuously carved. Close by, in the south aisle, is fine Arts and Crafts stained glass, designed by the painter and cartoonist Mary Lowndes, a founder of the Artists' Suffrage League, while Nicola Kantorowicz's 'Creation' stained glass in the west window, floods the crossing with rich colour. The Scott-tiled floor, perhaps one of the duller elements of the building, is at present being looked at with a view to replacing the nave portion with stone-flagged flooring, and removing the existing pews to recapture the open appearance of the original priory church.

BROOKLAND
St Augustine

he odd-shaped, free-standing 12th-century belfry at St Augustine's is the subject of much folklore in the Romney Marshes, but the truth is more prosaic. The church is built on unstable ground, with limited foundations, and additional forces generated by a belfry or tower would have pushed the church building beyond its stable limits.

Even without the weight of a tower, the nave arcades of St Augustine's lean tipsily in different directions. During construction, two internal flying

12th-century lead font

ously endowed with natural light from the 13th-century lancet windows in both north and south aisles, which run the full length of the nave and form two chapels at the northeast and southeast of the chancel. In the northeast chapel there are fragments of 14th-century stained glass, while, in the corner of the southeast chapel, is a 13th-century wall painting of the martyrdom of St Thomas à Becket, and the tomb of John Plomer, Baron of New Romney. The nave is full of box pews, and there is a good double-decker Georgian pulpit.

Most striking of all is the late-12th-century font, situated in the south aisle arcade. This is one of only thirty remaining lead fonts in the country, and is uniquely decorated. Two tiers of arcades, topped by bands of chevrons and braiding, enclose signs of the zodiac and the labours of the month; it is a simple but effective farming calendar.

buttresses were even added to support the arcades opening to the north aisle. The bell tower, with its three distinctive diminishing 'flounces', was originally an open framework, only enclosed by cladding in the 15th century.

The inside of the church is gener-

Nearby: Fairfield, St Thomas à Becket

CHURCH NORTON
St Wilfrid

The dedication of this lonely coastal chapel to St Wilfrid came late, in 1917. Before then, this former chancel of

the medieval Church of St Peter had been left stranded, after the church itself was moved to Selsey in the mid-19th century.

Although first impressions of St Wilfrid's are often of a chapel at the centre of a large cemetery, closer inspection clearly shows that St Wilfrid's was once part of something bigger. The Perpendicular window at the east end is suggestive of a much-larger church, and the buttressed west end has an overhanging gable, the apex of which is stepped out from the west wall and seems to symbolise the enforced separation of this chancel from its parent church. Inside, on the north wall is a 14th-century monument to John and Agas Lewis, whose pious kneeling figures are crudely carved into flanking sandstone panels. And, for the comfort of those volunteers who keep the church open, the floor is now covered with traditionally woven rush matting.

Nearby: Romsey, Romsey Abbey

COMPTON
Watts Cemetery Chapel

This profusely decorated chapel is an icon of the Arts and Crafts movement, and testimony to the self-improvement philosophy of the Home Arts and Industries Association.

Mary Watts and her husband George Frederic Watts, the Victorian painter and sculptor, were followers of the Home Art and Industries Association founded by the Irish-born social reformer Eglantyne Louisa Jebb. With typical Victorian rectitude Mary Watts invited villagers to her house in order to learn the craft of clay modelling and moulding. This offered opportunities for creative enlightenment and occupation to the villagers of Compton, thus turning their attention away from the temptations of Guildford's gin palaces.

In a moment of inspiration Mary Watts, taking advantage of an existing concern about overcrowding in the local churchyard and the subsequent purchase of a nearby piece of land for a new cemetery, offered to design and build a new cemetery chapel. The members of her clay classes were invited to produce decorations; seventy-four villagers took up the offer. The design was extraordinary: a confection of Celtic, Art Nouveau, Egyptian and Romanesque styles mixed in with Mary Watts's own personal style, and every element had symbolic meaning. It took three years to complete the exterior, and a further six years to finish the interior.

From a distance, the chapel peers over trees like a miniature Byzantine basilica. As one approaches, a profusion of detail snaps into focus: faces swathed in foliate swirls gaze sadly down, and corbels support a continuous frieze of angelic figures with sweeping wings, under which plaques enumerate virtues such as law, unity and truth. Below this is a frieze symbolising the Truth, the Way, and the Life, in which Celtic knots and Art Nouveau dragons' tails intermingle with abandon. A massive Romanesque doorway of three highly decorated orders frames a doorway of oak and chestnut, bearing a wrought-iron Ionian cross.

Inside, silver roots of the tree of life support groups of resplendent angels, illustrating all the fundamental states and their opposites – life and death, night and day, good and evil – and the domed ceiling is studded with a multitude of mystic gilded and vividly coloured medallions. It is a fusion of the elemental and the spiritual in well-heeled Surrey.

COOLING
St James CCT

In the churchyard, near the south porch, is a weathered headstone that watches over thirteen miniature tombstones, marking the burial places of thirteen infants from two families. It is a suitable, though unconfirmed, setting for the opening of Charles Dickens's novel *Great Expectations*: 'At such a time I found out for certain, that this bleak place overgrown with nettles was the churchyard ... and that the dark flat wilderness beyond the churchyard ... was the marshes.'

Visiting St James's Church on an early summer morning, it is hard to imagine the sinister landscape so vividly described: it is still isolated but, where there were marshes, there is now pasture, and, on the skyline, a sprawl of oil refineries. The church was built during the 13th and 14th centuries of local stone, mostly flint and Kentish ragstone. It is a grand building for such a small village. The diagonally buttressed tower with projecting stone staircase stands at the west end of a generously proportioned nave and chancel, and fine decorated windows are set at the east end and over the west doorway, a style continued in the north and south windows of the nave.

Excellent Early English stonework can be seen in the arcaded stone seats on the north and south chancel walls, and in the nave is a small group of medieval wooden benches, whose ends are ornamented with crude fleurs-de-lys terminations. There is a 13th-century font here too, of crudely square-cut ragstone resting on four corner shafts. To the south of the chancel is a tiny 19th-century vestry, whose walls are decorated from top to bottom with cockle shells; it is a whimsical tribute to the scallop shell symbol of the church's patron saint.

Nearby: Lower Higham, St Mary

DIDLING
St Andrew

This tiny church is known locally as the 'Shepherds' Church'; there are still hooks for the leashes of the shepherds' sheepdogs. St Andrew's is at the end of a farm track in a lonely spot: a place of wild flowers, bleating sheep and lark song. It is surrounded by open countryside, and sheltered from the south by the wooded slopes of the South Downs at whose feet it nestles. Outside is a plain churchyard with an old yew, and a scattering of 18th-century headstones.

The setting itself – evocative of simpler bygone times – is enough for a visit; this would have been a comfortless freezing church, with a care-worn and poor rural congregation.

St Andrew's was built sometime in the 13th century; it is a single-cell church, with rubble walls to the north and south, and rebuilt brick walls at the east and west ends. A simple stone bellcote stands at the apex of the west gable, and a crude wooden porch protects the north door. The bell is a recent arrival, replacing one stolen in recent years. Inside, the church is furnished with rough-hewn oak pews, and lit by simple 13th-century lancet windows. Opposite the north door is a tub font, said to be Saxon, but more likely 12th or 13th century. There is no electricity, only candlelight, and services are regularly held here.

ESHER
St George CCT

This little Tudor church, a cheerful jumble of sandstone rubble and brick originally built around 1540, is tucked behind the Bear Inn, off the High Street in Esher. It is a reminder of a time before the advent of the railways

Fairfield, St Thomas à Becket

HARDHAM
St Botolph

St Botolph's Church is set back from a now-bypassed section of road, which provides access only for the scattering of nearby houses and the church. This very early Norman, or possibly pre-conquest church, has one of the earliest surviving sets of medieval wall painting in England, all the more extraordinary for being in a minor church.

The paintings are part of the 'Lewes Group' work, produced by an itinerant group of artists in churches that were associated with the Cluniac priory of Lewes. Their other work in the locality can be seen at Clayton, Plumpton and Coombes. The paintings date from the early part of the 12th century, and closely resemble the style of the Bayeux Tapestry. Examples at

St Botolph's include paintings of: St George in battle; the adoration of the lamb; labours of the months; and, most striking of all on the west chancel wall, Adam and Eve. The technique is early fresco, in which plaster layers are painted while still wet. The colours were produced using a restricted range of locally available pigments: ochre, lime and carbon, and, rarely, malachite.

All the paintings have suffered from early crude attempts at preservation, including the application of size and varnish coatings in 1900, and wax in 1950. Consequently much detail was lost but, when one looks at the quality of what remains today, one can only speculate as to the magnificence of the paintings in their original state.

LONDON — CLERKENWELL
St Peter

The original conception of the 'La Chiesa Italiana di San Pietro a Londra' was of a Roman basilica church capable of accommodating some three-and-a-half-thousand people.

The idea came from Cardinal Wiseman, who asked an Italian priest of noble birth, Vincent Pallotti (later to be canonised for his work among the poor and sick, and for his efforts to revive the Catholic Church in England) to establish a church in the Clerkenwell area. An Italian community of about two thousand already existed, some working as street vendors, others working as artisans. An Irish architect Sir John Miller-Bryson drew up plans based on the Basilica of San Crisogono in Rome; these were modified to more modest dimensions and the church was consecrated in 1863. It was originally intended as a 'Church for all Nations', catering for congregations of differing nationalities, and, by the end of the century, was renowned for the quality of music, with orchestras and choirs regularly performing there.

The entrance to St Peter's – a loggia and double-arched portico set between offices and apartments – gives little clue to the rich interior. Polished marble columns with Corinthian capitals lead the eye through a triumphal chancel arch to the sanctuary, recessed under a half-domed ceiling with painted panels. Gilded-relief Corinthian pillars and fluted marble columns frame a magnificent painted reredos and lead the eye left and right to side altars. Above the nave are a series of blind arches, with paintings inset. This is a most sumptuous and invigorating expression of southern European Catholicism.

Nearby: London – Fleet Street, St Dunstan-in-the-West

LONDON – FLEET STREET
St Dunstan-in-the-West

Both Anglican and Romanian Orthodox congregations worship at St Dunstan's, one of the few churches in Britain to contain an iconostasis. The church is, however, best known for its clock – the first in London to have a minute hand and with two giants striking the hours – and the statues of King Lud and Elizabeth I in the courtyard.

It is said that the old church of St Dunstan's, which jutted out into Fleet Street, was pulled down after Londoners complained that it was interfering with traffic. It is more likely that the reason was a rebuilding necessitated by the passage of time. The architect John Shaw supervised his father's 1831 design of a new neo-Gothic exterior, crowned by an open lantern tower with fine tracery. This splendid Gothic exterior conceals an octagonal interior, which is divided

into chapel bays, highly appropriate for a church that prides itself on its ecumenical spirit. The Romanian Orthodox Church is represented here, as are the Armenian, Coptic, Ethiopian, Syrian, and Syro-Indian Oriental churches. Also represented is The Worshipful Company of Cordwainers. Many of the furnishings pre-date the 19th-century rebuilding and survived the Blitz.

Nearby: London – Clerkenwell, St Peter

Nearby: London – Clerkenwell, St Peter

LONDON — HAMPSTEAD
St John-at-Hampstead

An elegant avenue of 17th- and 18th-century houses leads to the beautiful Baroque Church of St John-at-Hampstead, a church whose align-ment was rotated on its axis and whose tower was saved after ferocious debate involving some of England's leading architects and artists.

In the mid-18th century the decision was taken to replace the decrepit wood and stone medieval church. The eminent architect Henry Flitcroft, whose works had included Burlington House and Woburn Abbey, submitted a design together with an offer of free services, as long as there was no competitive bid. The Trustees insisted on a competition, and, in a decision based on cost rather than quality, a local builder, John Sanderson, was chosen to rebuild the church. He moved the tower to the east end of the church.

During the 19th century Hampstead's popularity as a place of clean air drew an ever-increasing number of people to live in the village. By the 1870s it was decided that the church should be further enlarged at the west end, which would involve moving the altar from the east end, under the tower, to the enlarged west end. At the same time it was announced that the tower would be rebuilt: this provoked a fierce controversy involving the two competing architects for the scheme, Sir George Gilbert Scott and Frederick Cockerell. There were also lively interventions from a hastily formed Committee for the Preservation of the Tower of the Parish Church of St John-at-Hampstead, which included the architect Richard Norman Shaw, artist and stained-glass designer Henry Holiday, author and cartoonist George du Maurier and literary and art critic Sidney Colvin, as well as the Rossettis, Holman Hunt, and others from the art world. The objectors prevailed in the matter of the tower.

Today one can look west down Church Row and, if the church doors are open, see right through to the chancel at the west end of the church.

LONDON — LEICESTER PLACE
Notre Dame de France

The present church of Notre Dame de France, designed by the French architect Hector Corfiato, replaces Louis Auguste Boileau's remarkable iron church, destroyed in the Blitz. It is a modernist church, the façade of which is not to everyone's taste, but it represents a wide-ranging collaboration between architects, sculptors and artists.

On the façade above the entrance is a sculpture of the Virgin of Mercy by Georges Laurent Saupique, whose sculptures also adorn the Palais du

Trocadero in Paris. Inside, in the gallery, is a statue of Our Lady of Victories, an exact copy of the 15th-century sculpture in Paris's cathedral of Notre Dame. Having been badly damaged in the Blitz, the head was parachuted secretly into France, where the sculptor Henri Vallette used it to work out and remake the exact dimension of the rest of the figure. It became France's first post-war export to Britain.

In one of the chapels is an out-standing mural by the polymath Jean Cocteau, who was invited to take part in the redecoration of the new church by the French cultural attaché and academic Rene Varin. Cocteau responded by creating two murals: the Annunciation and the Crucifixion (above). These are wonderfully dynamic works, essentially linear with a strictly limited palette, demonstrating Cocteau's poetic passion for condensed meaning.

LONDON — PIMLICO
St Barnabas

St Barnabas was designed by Thomas Cundy Junior and Thomas Cundy III, who were both surveyors for the Grosvenor Estate. At the time of the church's construction in the 1850s Pimlico was a 'deplorable slum', far removed from today's elegance; this was a mission church.

The church embodied the principles of the Oxford Movement, formed by a group of High Anglican Oxford academics concerned about increased secularisation of the Church of England. They argued, in a series of tracts, for a return to apostolic order and the sacramental doctrines of the early Christian Church. St Barnabas's Church reflects these ideals in its recreation of Early English architecture and its sumptuous interior with fine Pre-Raphaelite decoration.

Stained-glass designer Charles Kempe, whose work can be also seen in Gloucester Cathedral and many other major churches, designed some of the stained glass. The capitals of the nave arcades are finely carved with scrolled foliage; delicate perpendicular tracery defines the rood screen, which in its turn supports a fine rood; the chancel arch and sanctuary ceiling are gilded and painted, while, behind the High altar, bedecked with fine candle-sticks by Augustus Pugin, is an outstanding and ornate carved reredos of the minutest detail.

Although it has only been in existence for 155 years, St Barnabas's is a good example of a church that has stayed architecturally true to itself, and stands to this day as a symbol of the principles of the Oxford Movement.

LOWER HIGHAM
St Mary CCT

Higham is made up of three villages descending a long slope that drops down to the edge of the Thames marshes, where, in Lower Higham, the ragstone and knapped flintstone Church of St Mary can be found. The church contains some outstanding medieval woodwork, in particular an ornately carved rood screen in its original position, and an excellent 14th-century carved wooden pulpit.

The striped appearance of the stonework at St Mary's owes its appearance to a technique in which irregular flints are cut with a flat face, and are set in such a way that the flat faces form a distinct horizontal band when set between courses of ragstone. This banding comes visually into its own when viewing the church from the west wall, as it accentuates the breadth of the double nave of St Mary's. Another ingenious use of flint can be seen on the southwest corner, where slivers have been inserted into the mortar.

The church is entered through an excellently preserved, wooden 15th-century door, exuberantly, if crudely, carved with a tracery design and decorated with roses and lilies and a variety of faces, including one of a very sleepy-looking monk. Between the chancel and the Lady Chapel – which was the chancel of the original Norman church – is a simple, carved 14th-century pulpit. Dividing the Lady chapel from the rest of the north aisle is a carved 15th-century wooden rood screen, composed of five Gothic arches, complete with Perpendicular wooden tracery. The centre arch forms a doorway; the screen originally supported a rood loft. Inside the screen

on a modern bier stands the 15th-century parish chest, a massive barrel-topped affair with iron strapping that would have contained church registers and other records, and, underneath, a 17th-century chest completely bound in iron strap work.

On the north wall, a 19th-century Tortoise stove recommends, with a cast iron motto, 'Slow but sure combustion'.

Nearby: Cooling, St James

MINSTEAD
All Saints

All Saints' Church dates from the 12th century, although it has been added to considerably. Small gabled extensions and gabled windows randomly inset in the pitch of the nave roof give it the appearance of a comfortable farm-house that has accidentally acquired a church tower: it has quaint charm.

The church is set back on a small rise behind the village green of Minstead, a small settlement on the edge of the New Forest. The chancel is set higher than the nave, and is divided from it by an 11th-century chancel arch that was very unsteadily improved in the 13th century. The

wooden furnishings bear witness to forest life: they are made from forest oak. A fine triple-decker pulpit and sturdy pews date from the 17th century. There are two galleries: the lower for the church band, a fine panelled affair; the upper, much plainer, for the local school children and the poor. A scattering of private pews with their own fireplaces for the gentry give a further domestic, if privileged, touch to this endearing church.

Admirers of Sherlock Holmes will undoubtedly come here to visit the grave of Sir Arthur Conan Doyle, and it is to be hoped that in their haste they don't neglect to visit the church itself.

Nearby: Romsey, Romsey Abbey

NEW ROMNEY
St Nicholas

The tower of St Nicholas's Church is one of Romney Marsh's most prominent landmarks. New Romney was one of the original Cinque Ports created by William the Conqueror, and St Nicholas's Church originally stood close to the harbour at the mouth of the River Rother.

New Romney's sea defences had been weakened by a series of fierce storms in the latter part of the 13th century, and, in 1287, the Great Storm overwhelmed the town and harbour, filling everywhere, including St Nicholas's Church, with silt and mud; the course of the River Rother was then changed, and, from being a coastal town, New Romney found itself a mile and a half from the sea.

Stains from the silt and mud can still be seen on some of the pillars in the church; the mud and silt from the Great Storm never having been fully cleared, the ground level of the church is at the original level of the surrounding land five feet below present street level. St Nicholas's Church was built by Odo, half-brother to William the Conqueror, between 1066 and 1087, making it the oldest church in the marshes, although this is contested by St Rumwold's. The tower, built slightly later, is lofty and impressive: the top four stages have Norman arcading, and the first stage has a finely ornamented west doorway, which was moved from the west end of the original nave to its present position.

There is an interesting transition of

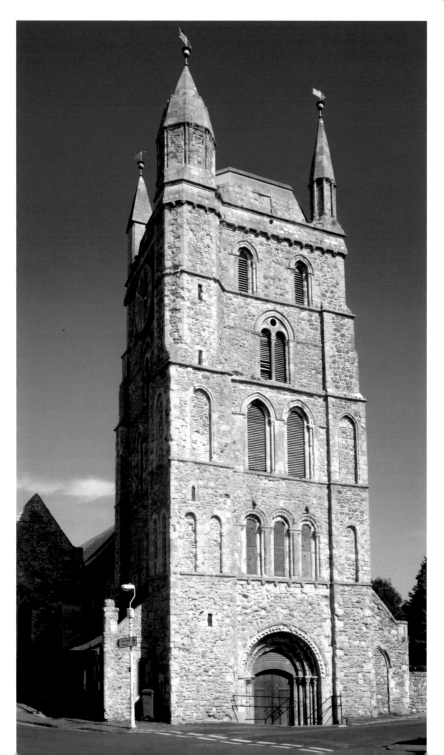

determined by the more practical issue of what to do with royal daughters – a succession of them took the veil here.

However, some striking Saxon stonework remains in and around the Norman abbey. Adjacent to the outside wall of the north aisle, and to the west of the north transept are the foundations of the Saxon porticus, while, by the abbess's door on the south wall sheltered by a modern canopy, is a

large relief carving of the crucified Christ with the hand of the Father reaching down from above, dating from the first part of the 11th century and in remarkable condition. It is thought to have been at the east end of the Saxon apse. In St Anne's chapel above the altar is another Saxon treasure, a carved Crucifixion scene. The detail is superb: Mary and St John stand at either side of the cross, which is giving forth tendrils symbolising new life. A Roman soldier thrusts a vinegar-soaked sponge towards Christ; the other thrusts a spear. It is thought that this carving was originally gilded, and may have been given to the nunnery by King Edgar in the 10th century.

Burial sites of three 9th-century Saxon nobles, together with rubble indicative of the footings of an even earlier Saxon church, were discovered in recent excavations to the north of the Saxon Abbey north transept.

Nearby: Minstead, All Saints

RUCKINGE
St Mary Magdalene

The Church of St Mary Magdalene stands on the 'Clay Hills', a slight rise on the northern fringes of the

Romney Marshes that separates them from the Weald of Kent. It is a stout church, whose tower acquired a new top stage in the 13th century.

The main building is of 12th-century origin, replacing an earlier Saxon church on the site. It has a fine twin-gabled termination to the east, with Geometrical–Curvilinear windows whose stone tracery has weathered badly. The aisle windows are mostly 14th century, and have traces of early glass in. One of the quatrefoils in the north aisle has a tantalising remnant of an angel standing on a leopard, which has been pierced through the mouth by a spear. In the window too are interesting remains of oak-leaf patterns, some in faint outline, and others more vividly in ochre.

The heavily weathered west door is Norman, as is a finely carved south door, with a chevron-patterned outer order, and a tessellated-pattern tympanum. Two mass sundials can be seen below and to the outside of the

responds. St Mary Magdalene's appears to be infrequently visited, which is a shame, as it is a good example of a no-nonsense country church with some interesting details.

ST MARY IN THE MARSH
St Mary the Virgin

There is a consistency between the architectural styles of many of the Romney Marsh churches, and St Mary the Virgin is no exception. Its short-shingled broach spire is very similar to that of St Clement's, its near neighbour. The children's author E Nesbitt is buried here, and a young Noel Coward lived in a cottage opposite the church.

St Mary the Virgin's started out as a small Norman church, and traces of Norman stonework can be seen beneath the tower arch and on its north side. The 13th century saw the con-

with the Purbeck marble font.

An unusual addition to the church was the Caryll Chapel, a chantry chapel added to the south of the chancel and used as a dame-school in the early 19th century before falling into ruins in 1860. A stone effigy of Sir Richard Caryll was left in the ruins until 1956, when it was placed in the south transept. It has weathered badly, but the stone ruff is a fine piece of carving. In the oppposite corner is the Cowper tomb, with its three painted figures.

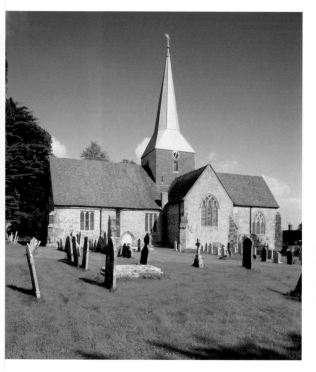

The churchyard gives fine views of the village and surrounding down-land. It also contains the burial place of Anthony Trollope, indefatigable chronicler of upper middle class Victorian England (his letter scales, pen and paperknife are displayed inside). A cross on a tall shaft, carved by sculptor and typographer Eric Gill, commemorates the dead from the Great War, and immediately outside the churchyard are the stocks and whipping post, complete with restraining wrist irons.

STOUGHTON
St Mary

This is a remarkably complete late Saxon church, built in the early part of the 11th century. Though hidden away on the southern slopes of the Downs and overlooked by ancient woodland, it is obviously valued by its parishioners, who keep it spotless and open for visitors.

The church follows a classic Saxon plan: high walls enclose a rectangular nave with small windows set high up. The Saxon nave and chancel windows

acquired their decorative mouldings and shafts during enlargement in the 12th and 13th centuries. The nave and chancel are connected by a high arch, giving an airy feel to the church. The chancel roof, however, is much lower than that of the nave, giving the north and south windows an abrupt, terminated appearance as the columns and mouldings now disappear into the roof. This resulted from remedial 16th-century work, when the builders found it cheaper and more expedient to re-move water-damaged top courses of masonry and lower the roofline rather than to rebuild to the original height.

The transepts were constructed in the 'porticus' chapel tradition, which permitted the burial of important persons close to the sanctuary but outside the nave. There were probably side altars in each transept, and over the south transept stands the tower, built over in the 14th century; a massive internal oak frame supports the bell chamber. The arches to both transepts were considerably enlarged towards the end of the 12th century.

Nearby: Bosham, Holy Trinity; Singleton, The Blessed Virgin Mary; Up Marden, St Michael

All Saints

The joy of All Saints' Church is its glass. A succession of 'hard' rebuilding and restorations of this medieval church have left nothing of great architectural interest; its present interior owes much to a good Victorian Gothic Revival restoration. However, it is hard to conceive of a parish church where 20th-century art has had such an impact, creating a church interior full of transcendental colour and light.

It was the tragic death of Sarah Venetia d'Avigdor-Goldsmid in a sailing accident in 1963 that led to the creation of All Saints' greatest asset, the Marc Chagall stained glass. Both Sarah and her mother were admirers of Chagall's work, and her father, Sir Henry d'Avigdor-Goldsmid, commissioned him to design a memorial window for the east chancel wall. The result is a deeply moving depiction of Sarah, mourned by grieving figures, floating on a swirl of waves, and, higher up the window, being led by a red horse – symbolic of happiness – to a ladder, at the top of which is the crucified Christ. The window is alive with movement and colour, and the chancel, flooded with its oceanic light, echoes the window.

Chagall himself was inspired by the results, and suggested that, if it were not for the remaining stained glass in the church, he would happily do all the windows. Sir Henry took up his offer, commissioning Chagall to submit designs for all the remaining windows. The nave windows were completed by the end of the 1960s, and the remaining chancel windows were installed, after some reservations by parishioners concerning the siting of the old stained glass were resolved by backlighting them with a lightbox in the vestry.

The church is suffused with colour from the windows: golds and ochres from the south; marine blues from the chancel; purple, aquamarine and greens from the north aisle. This is 20th-century church art at its most expressive and moving.

The east chancel memorial window

UP MARDEN
St Michael

There are two ways of approaching St Michael's Church: down a rough track from a nearby lane; or by footpath through neighbouring fields. The church stands in a churchyard full of leaning headstones, and is celebrated neither for its architecture nor furnishings – of which there are virtually none – but rather for its ascetic rural simplicity and spirituality. But what is it about St Michael's that marks it out as different? Journalist and author Simon Jenkins imagines labourers from the fields around finding comfort and solace here, while guidebook authors Ian Nairn and Nikolaus Pevsner write of 'an atmosphere as tangible as any moulding'.

It is a church in its most basic form, an unselfconscious building, divided into chancel and nave by a triangular archway that was thought to be Saxon, and now is thought to be an emergency repair from the 16th century. The floors are brick and the pews are plain, except for a small number of box pews inside the chancel for those who thought themselves better, and over whose use the church's tranquillity is said to have been disrupted by the occasional violent disagreement. A small touch of gaiety that adds to the ambience of the church hangs above: cheerful blue and gilded candelabra illuminate the nave and chancel.

Nearby: Bosham, Holy Trinity; Singleton, The Blessed Virgin Mary; Stoughton, St Mary the Virgin

Central and Eastern England

East Anglia is the land of water and fen, of big skies and limitless horizons, whose great era of church building and rebuilding took place in the 15th century. Flint was the predominant material and yet, with such poor quality building material, Perpendicular architecture in Suffolk and Norfolk reached its most expressive.

Towers and spires are the overriding feature of the church landscape in the east, from the great Victorian gothic spire of St Mary the Virgin at Saffron Walden, the flying buttresses of Thaxted's St John's Church, distinctive round towers of Norfolk and Suffolk to, far to the north, the Rhenish Towers of Southwell Minster – Normandy in Nottinghamshire.

Somewhat overshadowed by the great Perpendicular wool churches are many modest but delightful gems. Nicholas Ferrars' church at Little Gidding has a Baroque façade and an exquisite wood-panelled interior. St John's Church in Duxford is in a delightful village green setting, while Suffolk's most extensive Iron Age fort is the setting for St Botolph's in Burgh, whose site was said to be the home of a marsh-dwelling demon.

In the extreme southwest, tucked away in the Chiltern village of Fingest is St Bartholomew's, with its distinctive and highly unusual double saddleback roof. Norman architecture at its best can be seen at St Michael's in Stewkley, while the nearby church of All Saints' at Wing is an outstanding example of Anglo Saxon architecture, with a fine crypt and polygonal apse.

St Mary Magdalene in Willen is a graceful and elegant example of Georgian architecture, holding its own against the surge of Milton Keynes suburbs, but the most intriguing church in this section is All Saints' in Earls Barton. Outside the tower has some of the finest Anglo Saxon decorative stonework in the country, while, inside, a fine Perpendicular rood screen is painted with clouds of moths and butterflies, the work of a scene painter at the Old Vic theatre.

List of Churches

Acle, St Edmund King & Martyr
Aldworth, St Mary the Virgin
Badingham, St John the Baptist
Bessingham, St Mary
Blundeston, St Mary
Blythburgh, Most Holy Trinity
Bradwell-on-Sea, St Peter-on-the-wall
Burgh, St Botolph
Crowland, Croyland Abbey
Denston, St Nicholas
Duxford, St John
Earls Barton, All Saints
Fingest, St Bartholomew
Haddiscoe, St Mary
Little Gidding, St John

Little Kimble, All Saints
Nether Winchendon, St Nicholas
Saffron Walden, St Mary the Virgin
Southwell, Southwell Minster
Stewkley, St Michael and All Angels
Thaxted, St John the Baptist,
    Our Lady and St Laurence
Thornham Parva, St Mary
Waddesdon Hill, Waddesdon Strict &
    Particular Baptist Chapel
Walpole, Walpole Old Chapel
Westhall, St Andrew
Willen, St Mary Magdalene
Wing, All Saints

SOUTHWELL

BESSINGHAM

ACLÉ

BLUNDESTON

CROWLAND

WESTHALL · HADDISCOE

LITTLE GIDDING

THORNHAM PARVA

WALPOLE · BLYTHBURGH

BADINGHAM

EARLS BARTON

BURGH

DUXFORD · DENSTON

WILLEN · SAFFRON WALDEN

STEWKLEY

THAXTED

WING

NETHER WINCHENDON

LITTLE KIMBLE · WADDESTON HILL

BRADWELL-ON-SEA

ALDWORTH FINGEST

ACLE
St Edmund King and Martyr

St Edmund's Church has a distinctive Norfolk round tower and Norfolk reed-thatched nave roof; inside is an outstanding 15th-century font.

This is a fine church, an oasis of calm next to and surrounded by busy roads in the town centre. The round tower is topped by a 13th-century octagonal stage, embattled with pinnacles, one of which is dedicated to St Edmund, the 9th-century King of East Anglia. A sturdy wagon-roof covers the nave, and the chancel arch has a fine and delicately carved Perpendicular rood screen; the lower part is painted, and ornamented with a motif symbolising Edmund's martyrdom. Although the rood is modern, its simplicity is in keeping with the original screen.

The octagonal 15th-century font is at the west end of the nave; it is a magnificent piece of carving that survived the iconoclasts' zeal and subsequent plastering over. The Victorians removed the plaster, uncovering the eight relief panels, which depict the Evangelists, angels, and the Virgin with the dead Christ. Some of the vandalised faces were restored by the Victorians, but with sensitivity, and, more remarkably, some of the original colouring survives.

ALDWORTH
St Mary the Virgin

St Mary's Church is in the Berkshire
Downs, close to the site of the De La
Beche family's castle. Buried in the
churchyard are the poet Laurence
Binyon and the parents-in-law of
Alfred, Lord Tennyson.

Inside the church are an outstanding group of 14th-century effigies
known as the Aldworth Giants. All
nine of the figures were members of
the De La Beche family, making this a
unique collection, even more so as
there is much detail on the costumes
and accoutrements. The largest of the
figures is Sir Philip De La Beche, son
of Sir John, seven feet in length and
whose size is emphasised by a dwarf-
like figure at his feet. The figure in the
centre of the nave is thought to be Sir
Nicholas De La Beche, Seneschal of
Gascony and Constable of the Tower of
London; he has wonderful, detailed
stitching on his garments. The double

effigy is that of Sir John and Lady
Isabella De La Beche.

Elizabeth I is believed to have come
to St Mary's in company with the Earl
of Leicester to view the Aldworth
Giants; the Giants were later damaged
during the English Civil War.

BADINGHAM
St John the Baptist

St John's is a mostly 13th-century
church in a quiet Suffolk village. It has
an unusual ascending slope from the

west to the east end of the nave, the
late 15th-century font has outstanding
sacramental carvings, and there is a

very fine roof. The most interesting feature of the exterior of St John's is an ornate 15th-century porch, whose south façade is ornamented with flint flush-work. A dragon and wildman are carved on the spandrels above the door, and on the diagonal buttresses are some delightful carvings – on the east buttress is a carving of a crouching hound with a bowl in its mouth. The corbels inside the porch are interesting too: a very cheerful cat, and a man holding his head.

Inside, the nave has a narrow, high feeling, more typical of Saxon churches; the nave slopes upwards to the chancel, which was restored in a rather gloomy style in the 19th century. And over the nave is a superb single hammerbeam roof, whose carved angels are Victorian, replacing 'superstitious cherubim' that had been destroyed by the infamous 17th-century Suffolk iconoclast William Dowsing. Though not the most ornate or beautiful example of its type, the roof (left) is considered by some, including Henry Cautley, early 20th century diocesan architect and author of *Suffolk Churches and Their Treasures*, to be the best technical example of single hammerbeam construction in England.

The late 15th-century sacramental font is the most compelling furnishing in St John's. It is octagonal in form and the carvings on each panel have intimate detail: in the Last Rites the dying man's shoes and chamber pot can be seen under the bed; the Consecration panel shows the sanctus bell being held by one server, while two heads peep from behind the reredos; on the Penance panel a fiend is being expelled by the act of absolution; while the infant on the Baptism panel is being dipped with a certain amount of maternal caution.

Nearby: Walpole, Walpole Old Chapel

BESSINGHAM
St Mary

This outstanding example of a Saxon round tower church is deep in the Norfolk countryside south of Cromer; it is remote, rural and hard to find.

A sensitive restoration by Charles Eamer Kempe and the London workshops of John Powell and Sons has left that most unusual of legacies at St Andrew's – good Victorian stained glass. The nave and chancel are effectively a complete Victorian rebuilding, but a very good one. It would have been so easy to spoil such a simple little church, the appeal of which is in its general appearance rather than the fittings and furnishings. Instead, the nave and chancel are flooded with beautiful light from the south windows. There are no aisles, just a tall narrow nave and chancel of Saxon proportions; high in the west wall of the nave is a Saxon doorway, leading into the intact Saxon round tower. The tower is in excellent condition and complete with its triangular headed bell chamber openings. The only addition has been some extra courses of flint, and a brick-tiled battlement.

The difference between the flint and the different stages of stone used in the lower stages of the tower marks the development of the tower, and the church itself is not, as is customary, built of flint or rubble, but of carstone, a warmer type of stone from the west of Norfolk.

BLUNDESTON
St Mary

Charles Dickens used the village of 'Blunderstone' as the birthplace of his eponymous hero David Copperfield, in the novel of the same name. In the novel, David Copperfield says of St Mary's, 'There is nothing half so green that I know anywhere, as the grass of that churchyard; nothing half so shady as its trees; nothing half so quiet as its tombstones.'

Today St Mary's is still sheltered by trees, though the sheep-farming landscape has long given way to vast, prairie-like arable fields. The church has an interesting late 10th-century round tower, oddly attached off-axis

to the nave. There is a change of masonry halfway up, and again just under the bell openings. It is worth looking at the windows: the lowest window is from the 15th or 16th century, made of brick; further up at the first change of masonry are small 12th-century lancet windows; at the level of the apex of the nave gable is a series of blocked-up arched windows – the original bell openings. Interspersed with them are more 12th-century lancet windows, and, at the top, 12th-century bell openings.

The original Norman nave and chancel were replaced in the 14th century by a larger building that is mostly intact, notwithstanding a Victorian restoration during which the chancel was rebuilt. The Curvilinear stone tracery in the nave windows is of very good quality, and the church has re-tained its carved wooden rood screen, which dates from 1490. The pews are all Victorian, although the restorers had the forethought to reuse the 14th-century poppy-head bench ornaments where possible.

Nearby: Haddiscoe, St Mary

BLYTHBURGH
Most Holy Trinity

The first glimpse of Holy Trinity Church is startling: a grand stately building, surrounded by marshes and overlook-ing the River Blyth, it is isolated from its small village by an alarmingly busy main road. So how did such a magnif-icent church come to be built in such an apparently out-of-the-way setting?

The generally accepted explanation once was that Blythburgh was once a busy medieval town and therefore needed a large church. This is unlikely, as the new church was built during a period of steep economic decline in the area. Rather, the impetus to build a new church came from the prior of

BURGH
BURGH
St Botolph

Burgh is Suffolk's largest Iron Age fort, dating from the 1st century BC; it was the regional centre of commerce, administration and religion. St Botolph's Church sits on an ancient mound, believed in the Dark Ages to be the home of a demon. Perhaps this demon was something like Beowulf's marsh-dwelling monster; as late as the 7th century, attempts were being made to

exorcise it. The dedication to St Botolph would have been apt, as he enjoyed a reputation as an exorcist of marsh monsters. His remains spent some years at the church before being moved to Bury Abbey.

The church itself is a mixture of Decorated and Perpendicular architecture, and has a south tower, and on the south door is a 13th-century sanctuary knocker. The idea of being able to claim sanctuary in a church dates back to the reign of King Ethelbert, in the 5th century: a person who had committed a crime, or who was fleeing from persecution, could claim the protection of the church. In the case of a criminal, crimes could be confessed and an oath taken to leave the realm, and, in the case of persecution, the protection of the church against the secular authorities could be sought. The practice came to an end under Henry VIII.

CROWLAND
Croyland Abbey

Despite the setback of being destroyed three times – once by the Danes and twice by fire – Croyland Abbey in Lincolnshire was a prosperous

Benedictine foundation up until the dissolution, after which Edward VI granted the lands and monastic buildings to Edward, Lord Clinton. In the English Civil War the abbey was occupied by Royalist forces in 1643, then besieged and overrun by the Parliamentarians later in the same year.

The nave and south aisle are now in ruins, and only the skeletal outline of the west front remains standing, still with the statues of saints in niches over the great west window. What has remained intact is the north aisle, which has been in parish use since the 15th century and continues to function as the parish church.

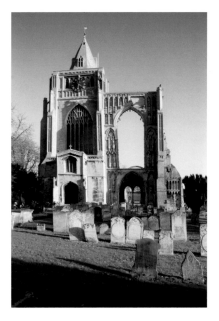

DENSTON
St Nicholas CCT

This is a church that celebrates the art of the woodcarver; carved bench-ends, misericords and the roof all bear witness to craftsmanship and imagination.

With the exception of the tower, St Nicholas's Church was entirely rebuilt by John Denston in the 15th century as a collegiate church. It is a fine example of late Perpendicular architecture at its simplest, with a long nave and chancel all in one space.

Carved animals – manticores (monsters with the head of a human,

the body of a lion and the tail of a scorpion), hares and hounds – bound along the wall plates of the roof, the wood faded to a pale whitish grey colour; underneath, in the nave, is an almost complete set of medieval benches whose ends are also decorated with a wonderful set of carved animals. Some of their origins seem to be derived from the medieval bestiary – the cockatrice (a dragon-winged creature with a cock's head and serpent's tail), the lion, numerous

rabbits, and a rather charming elephant made up of the right parts in the wrong order – and is clearly the result of received description rather than direct observation. There is also a fine piece of stone carving in the church – a 15th-century sacramental font, whose panels have been hacked at by the iconoclasts of the Reformation.

An odd feature of some of the windows in the west aisles is that the lower halves have been bricked up during an 18th-century attempt to conserve heat in the church.

DUXFORD
St John CCT

St John's Church has the most delightful village-green setting, surrounded by cottages. It has been disused, but not neglected, since 1870.

This is a substantial village church whose fabric has Norman, Early English, Decorated and Perpendicular styles, which are reflected in the differing materials used. These include Cambridgeshire cobbles, Northamp-tonshire limestone, clunch (a chalky clay based rock often quarried from open fields), and Tudor and Stuart brickwork.

Inside St John's all is air and space. Furnishings are restricted to a few rough-carved 14th-century benches in the nave, a plain 17th-century pulpit and Laudian communion rails. The emptiness conveys a striking impression of the church as it was before the introduction of seating. A progression from Norman in the nave and tower, to the Early English of the chancel, the Decorated in the north chapel, and Perpendicular of the north aisle invite an informative walk through the progression of church architecture from the conquest to the 15th century. The Decorated tracery in the east window of the north chapel is particularly fine.

On the chancel walls and arch are 12th- and 13th-century wall paintings – these are still in the process of being uncovered, but visible images include scenes from the Crucifixion and saints; in the north aisle, fragmentary traces of 15th-century wall paintings can be seen on the north wall.

Nearby: Saffron Walden, St Mary the Virgin

EARLS BARTON
All Saints

As well as having a tower that is one of the most interesting examples of late Anglo Saxon architecture in the country, All Saints' contains a fascinating Perpendicular screen, redecorated in the 1930s.

The tower – a fine example of Anglo Saxon decorative work – has interlaced strips of stone called lesenes that run from the base to the top in straight lines. They form a semicircular motif at the base of the second stage, while a more elaborate triangular pattern dec-

orates the third stage. The bell openings on the fourth stage are formed of a colonnade of slightly bulging columns supporting round arches.

Above a rudimentary window and under the clock face is a doorway, possibly permitting controlled access to the upper part of the tower in times of danger. The space inside the base of the tower, however, may have been part of the early church.

The south doorway, with its leaning columns and beak-head decoration is

Norman, as are the blind arcades in-side, but the most commanding sight inside the church is the Perpendicular rood screen. Henry Bird, a member of the Society of Mural Painters and head scene painter at the Old Vic and Sadler's Wells theatres, painted this in 1935. Clouds of butterflies and moths on a sky-blue background ornament the fan-vaulted coving, while saints in contemporary dress are painted on the lower panels. At the time the church authorities thought it sacrilegious; the parishioners thought otherwise and the paintings stayed.

FINGEST
St Bartholomew

The massive tower of the Church of St Bartholomew, with its rough-cast ochre colour, is set at the edge of the picturesque village of Fingest, and is a familiar sight to walkers in the nearby Chiltern hills.

This attractive Norman church is distinguished by the unusual double saddleback roof of its tower. This is a very unusual feature for a Norman tower in England; the sheer girth of the tower – which is about one third wider than the body of the church – is also unusual. Norman towers were more usually built centrally, between the chancel and the nave; St Bartholomew's tower, as at the church of St Michael with St Mary at Melbourne in Derbyshire, is at the west end. The tower rises in a single unbroken stage, and has well-carved bell chamber lights at the top. The main window in the west wall of the tower is from the 14th century, with Decorated tracery.

The nave is tall and narrow – one continuous space with the chancel – giving it an almost Saxon appearance. Impressive rafters and tie-beams support the roof. The chancel is of a slightly later date than the nave – 13th century – and it is possible that it replaced an earlier apse.

HADDISCOE
St Mary

A chequered pattern, 15th-century stage crowns the round tower of St Mary's; this slim tower looks out over a watery landscape of marshes and the River Waveney. The base of the tower is Saxon, the upper stages Norman, and above the south doorway is a fine Norman relief carving, variously thought to be either Christ in Majesty, or St Peter.

Inside, the church is a little dim: some light filters in from the south aisle windows and from the east chancel window, but the north aisle – which seems to be a bit of an afterthought – is less well-endowed with windows. There are a double piscina and two corbels in the chancel, and a faint wall painting of St Christopher can be seen on the north wall.

Nearby: Blundeston, St Mary

LITTLE GIDDING
St John

In the 17th century, having nearly been ruined by the collapse of the Virginia Company – a company set up to establish an English settlement in the Chesapeake region of North America, and which had its charter revoked following the Indian Massacre of 1622 and mismanagement at home – Nicholas Ferrar and his widowed mother Mary decided to leave London, and to turn to a life of religious devotion. The family bought the Manor of Little Gidding, in Cambridgeshire, but an outbreak of the plague brought about an earlier than intended move from London to Little Gidding, where they found both the manor house and 12th-century church in ruins.

Such was Mary Ferrar's devotion that she ordered the church to be repaired and brought into good order before the house. In due course, other members of the family joined them, increasing the household to 40 people. Led by Nicholas Ferrar, who had been ordained as a deacon by Archbishop Laud, a religious community developed. It was organised around a rigorous timetable of vigils, prayer, gospel and psalm readings; the community was also busy bookbind-

ing, and dispensing alms and medicine. The death of John Ferrar in the mid-17th century marked the end of the community, although his descendants renovated the church during the first part of the 18th century, a process completed by William Hopkinson, then owner of a new manor house, in 1853.

The church is diminutive, and its original two-cell plan was retained by Ferrar's 17th-century rebuilding. Wooden choir stall seating lines both sides of the nave, and wood panelling joins a wooden barrel-vaulted roof.

SOUTHWELL

Southwell Minster

Southwell Minster is one of England's magnificent curiosities: a great and beautiful cathedral but often missed, looking over fields and a tiny market town. The fine Norman west front is crowned with twin pyramidal Rhenish spires and gives the impression that one has accidentally strayed into Normandy.

Southwell Minster has retained many of its original Norman characteristics. The 12th-century west door, surrounded by characteristic dog-tooth carving, opens on to a magnificent Norman nave, with monolithic round pillars supporting three tiers of half-rounded arches rising to a Victorian timber wagon-roof. The principal impression is one of simplicity and light, two features that in turn combine to create a pervading sense of peace.

The Minster has a multitude of features worth exploring but the carvings in the chapter house and on the quire screen are particularly noteworthy. The chapter house is a superb example of the Early English style, dating from the end of the 13th century, and its profuse and renowned carvings are known as the 'Leaves of Southwell'. Ten green men, vines sprouting from their mouths, can be seen among this exuberant outpouring of imagination, which moves over arches and capitals, corbels, crockets and finials, vaulting, shafts and bosses in a profusion of creatures, human caricatures, leaves, fruit and flowers from fields, hedgerows and forests.

No fewer than 286 carved figures

also look out from the Decorated stone pulpitum: kings and queens, nobles and knights, bishops and priests, tradesmen and craftsmen. All are ranked in social order from top to bottom; scattered here and there the mason's sense of humour is evident in caricatures, a bottom scratched here, a chin being stroked pensively there.

St Michael and All Angels

Of the 6,000 or so churches built by the Normans in England, St Michael's is one of a very few to have survived to its original plan.

The church dances with decoration: zigzag decoration surrounds the three orders of the west doorway and its flanking blind arcades; a braided string-course flows round the top of the doorway. Above is a Norman window, similarly decorated, whose sill also follows the same contour. The tympanum, ornamented with dragons, is unusually interrupted by a hanging keystone.

The interior is divided into three – nave, tower and chancel – and each is separated by carved arches, the most splendid of which is the chancel arch. The inner order is carved with beak-head images, one of which is a trio of monkey faces. Vigorous double chevrons zigzag round the second order, with a similar but finer pattern ornamenting the outmost order.

The chancel roof is rib-vaulted, and even the ribs are decorated with double chevrons, as are all the window surrounds and the internal string-course.

In 1970 the Roskill Commission was looking into the implications of siting a third London airport in the area, and it was suggested that St Michael's Church be dismantled and rebuilt elsewhere. A bag of rubble in-fill was presented to the commission to demonstrate that, if such a dismantling was attempted, the church walls would disintegrate. The airport was built elsewhere; St Michael's thankfully stayed put.

Nearby: Wing, All Saints

THAXTED
St John the Baptist with Our Lady and St Lawrence

Thaxted church has been described as the best parish church in England; although there may be those that contest that title, St John's Church is a remarkable building and an expression of Anglo-Catholicism rich in

medieval carvings, light and space.

Built between 1349 and 1510, Thaxted church is one of the Perpendicular wonders of East Anglia, with a magnificent interior, which is a harmonious blend of architectural styles and in which the aisles, broader than the nave, are almost as wide as the transepts. The arcades create rich patterns, both in the nave and in the chancel, which has its own aisles. Fine windows let light flood through the church, creating a fascinating interplay of light and shade in the crossing. The detail in the stonework is inspiring: from the open spandrels in the chancel arcades, to the riot of gargoyles, angels and religious figures of every sort that spread throughout the church.

The church owes much to the

colourful Conrad Noel, vicar at Thaxted until 1942; he was a Christian Socialist, architectural purist and radical liturgist who once flew the Red Flag in church as a symbol of internationalism and social justice. He revived a medieval sense of pageantry and his curate Jack Putterill, later to be known as 'the other Red Vicar' of Thaxted, maintained his traditions.

THORNHAM PARVA
St Mary

St Mary's is a little thatched Norman church sited in a field deep in the Suffolk countryside; its charming but modest appearance (see following page) gives no hint of the richness of its contents.

Artists in the 14th century used the nave walls of St Mary's to create what has become one of the county's most interesting collections of wall paintings: there are two main groups of pictures, both containing a narrative. Starting in the southwest corner is a series of paintings illustrating the Visitation – the appearance of the angel to the shepherds – and the presentation in the temple. The very first painting in the series has not survived, but is assumed to have been of the Annunciation. The second group of paintings continues on the north nave wall: a 1970s restoration revealed that the series on this wall, originally thought to illustrate the martyrdom of St Catherine, depicts the story of the martyrdom of St Edmund. The colours are faded, windows interrupt some of the pictures, the gallery cuts into a painting of the bullock cart carrying St Edmund's corpse, and some of the pictures have been entirely lost, but this is still a remarkable set of medieval wall paintings.

In better repair is the impressive retable, found in a nearby barn in the 1920s. This is a section of a much larger retable rescued from Thetford Priory after the Reformation. At the centre is Christ crucified, and on either side are saints, painted with vigour and dynamism; the folds of material in the clothing have fine flowing movement.

The 20th century has made its contribution with etched glass by Laurence Whistler: graceful flowers and inspirational sunrises are set into the medieval windows.

WADDESDON HILL, NEAR WADDESDON
Waddesdon Strict and Particular Baptist Church FoFC

This chapel stands on a windswept hill-top, its austere simplicity an expression of the movement for which it was founded in 1792 by Francis Cox – the Strict and Particular Baptists. Baptists believe that, after conversion, believers should be immersed in water as part of their profession of faith; in the late 18th century, when this chapel was founded, total immersion baptism had become a well-established practice with both the General and Particular Baptists. In Waddesdon chapel, there is a total immersion font under the floor. Men who were baptised thus were expected to bear the cold without complaint, but a separate room with a fireplace was provided for women.

The Strict and Particular Baptists followed a Calvinist view of particular atonement – only the elect would be saved. They also maintained a strict position on membership and com-munion: the communion table was restricted to baptised believers. Strict and Particular Baptists believe that the Lord's Supper is a divine ordinance, to be celebrated only by a congregation comprised of saved and baptised believers.

To see Waddesdon on a sunny day, it is hard to imagine the ordeal such a baptism must have been in a cold winter.

Nearby: Nether Winchendon, St Nicholas

Walpole Old Chapel нст

It was not until after the Act of Toleration in 1689 that Walpole Old Chapel was founded within a 16th-century farmhouse. Though it still looks like a domestic building on the outside, the inside is one of the oldest dissenters' chapels in England.

In 1649 a group of dissenters, fired by their conviction of predestined salvation and their determination to reject any external authority, established themselves at Walpole. The leaders were self-styled 'saints' – alumni of Emmanuel College, Cambridge, a bastion of Puritanism. The interior, converted after the Act of Toleration, reflects the 18th-century popularity of the chapel, from which time it has been virtually unchanged. Georgian box pews for the better-off occupy the ground floor, while galleries accommodated the poorer members of the congregation. There is no altar, no cross: the emphasis was on the teaching of the Word, and all the seats in the chapel are aligned to face a two-decker pulpit on a raised platform against the north wall. The reader and elders sat on the first level; the second was reserved for the preacher. In the centre of the chapel a stout timber – said to be a mast from a ship-breakers in Southwold – supports the roof.

Nearby: Badingham, St John the Baptist

St Andrew

St Andrew's is a paradox. The present south aisle was the original nave of an early Norman church, the magnificent west entrance of which is now enclosed

by a 13th-century west tower; the east
face of the tower still bears the gable
outline of an earlier roof. In the 13th
century, a thatched north aisle was
added to the old nave, on to which a
new chancel was built in the 14th
century. This is almost like two churches
from different periods, side by side.
There is an entry through the 14th-
century porch on the north side, or by
the Norman doorway on the south.

To see the Norman west doorway,
one has to enter the space under the
tower: this is a five-order round-
arched doorway with exuberant
Romanesque carving. Of particular
interest are the carved heads on the
fourth order: upturned moustaches;
pendulous noses; cats' ears; and
protruding tongues run round the
arch in a mischievous parade of
grotesque sculptures. The south doorway, while simpler, also has fine decorative carving, particularly in the
unbroken hood-mould.

All this is simply a prelude to what
awaits inside, however: a panelled and
painted rood screen dating from around
1500, wall paintings and a vividly
coloured sacramental font. The figures
on the rood screen, though crudely
executed, possess a compelling vitality
of colour, expression and composi-
tion: St Clement holds an anchor; St
James is attired as a Compostela pilgrim;
and, rather more faded and painted by

a different artist, are St Agnes and
St Apollonia, the patron saint of
toothache sufferers. Most remarkable
of all are the three panels depicting
the Transfiguration, possibly the only
remaining example in England.

The sacramental font is one of
several in Suffolk, but is notable for its
retention of colour. Though defaced,
the carvings still show a considerable
amount of detail, and sufficient paintwork has survived to show patterning
on material, as well as lettering and
skin tone. The best-preserved parts of
painting are on the rim of the font,
and the carved panel surrounds. The
wall paintings, faded and fragmentary
though they are, are also of interest,
particularly that of Moses receiving
the Ten Commandments.

St Mary Magdalene

In the 1960s Willen was a small
Buckinghamshire village by the River
Ouzel, with only a church and
vicarage, two large farms, a scattering
of cottages and the remnants of a watermill. Now it is a larger district, to

which the old village gives its name,
but the church, a fine Restoration
classical building, is still there on a
small rise, resisting the nondescript
tide of housing that surrounds it.

St Mary's was designed and built in

about 1680 for Dr Busby, headmaster of Westminster School, by Robert Hooke, a former pupil of Westminster, and the Royal Society's Secretary and Curator of Experiments. The original building was a rectangular chamber and west tower, to the north and south side of which vestries were added shortly after – carelessly as it transpires; the brickwork was not bonded to the tower and nave, giving rise to structural problems. In 1861 an apsidal chancel was added at the east end, and, in 1988, the interior acquired a new colour scheme, replacing the original blue and white paintwork.

The interior is barrel-vaulted, complemented well by the domed apse ceiling. There is a fine marble font carved with cherubs with an intricately carved wooden font cover. The ceiling is adorned with white plaster relief work, and inset dusty-pink panels, in the centre of which is a gilded plaster boss. The nave has simple box pews and the original wall panelling, while the organ, thought to have come from Dr Busby's home, sits opposite the pulpit. This is a most attractive church, tastefully maintained by its small number of parishioners.

WING
All Saints

An imposing polygonal Anglo Saxon apse juts out like a blunted ship's bow from the east end of All Saints', built over an Anglo Saxon crypt. The presence at All Saints' of an 8th-century crypt and 9th-century apse, combined with the tall narrow Saxon nave and aisles is quite exceptional, and the only example of its kind in England. The crypt was opened in 1878 in the course of restoration work.

All Saints' has retained much of its Saxon simplicity. Not until the 14th century were changes made to its

structure, when the south aisle was added. This was followed in the 15th century by the rebuilding of the tower, and the construction of the south porch and fine carved oak roof with back-to-back angels on the trusses. There are some conspicuous monuments in the church, particularly that of the High Sheriff of Bedfordshire and Buckinghamshire, Sir Robert Dormer, and an altar tomb with carved bulls' head on the front panel (overleaf), flanked by pairs of extravagant Corinthinian columns. In the chancel, and only slightly more restrained, are monuments to Robert's son Sir William Dormer and family, and a later Robert Lord Dormer and his family. On a much more human scale is a memorial brass on the south wall to: 'HONEST OLD THOMAS COTES, THAT SOMETIME WAS PORTER AT ASCOTT HALL, HAT NOW (ALAS!) LEFT HIS KEY, LODGE, FURE, FRIENDS AND ALL TO HAVE A ROOM IN HEAVEN'.

Nearby: Stewkley, St Michael

Western England

This section is a liberal interpretation of western England, encompassing churches from Derbyshire, Warwickshire, Herefordshire and Worcestershire. The architectural styles of the churches included here are very varied, with the exception of Anglo Saxon, of which there is very little, particularly in Herefordshire.

As Herefordshire is the setting for my initial interest in churches, the county's churches are heavily represented. This is an area of constantly changing light, of deep red soil and sandstone churches. Of all the English counties, it alone offers no easy passage through to anywhere else: there are no motorways, only a network of roads and lanes that serve a mainly rural population, and the churches sit well in their landscapes. There is a rich tradition of Norman architecture and Romanesque sculpture here, as well as some oddities – the 'Strawberry Hill Gothick' of St John the Evangelist at Shobdon, and the appalling fibreglass spire of St Peter's Church in Peterchurch, which also, unusually for the county, has outstanding Anglo Saxon features.

Derbyshire's churches are in stark contrast to this: the county was once the Saxon kingdom of Mercia, and the great Anglo Saxon treasure here is St Wystan's in Repton. Further north in the Peak District, churches have a more sombre aspect, with embattled naves

BROMSBERROW
St Mary

This is a modest little parish church on the Herefordshire–Gloucestershire border, whose timbered tower and broach spire peep over a surrounding screen of trees. Its origins are late 12th century, and the peaceful graveyard contains the burial places of two brothers of the poet John Masefield.

The oldest part of the church is the tower: three Early English lancet windows pierce the first sandstone stage. The half-timbered third stage and broach steeple are rather charming Victorian additions. The nave shows signs of Victorian rebuilding, with a new south wall and pleasant wooden, arched wagon roof. Two hatchments to the Yates family can be seen on the south wall, and a plain Norman tub font is situated at the west end. The chancel is largely medieval, with a well-proportioned chancel arch and very attractive curvilinear window at the east end, with replacement Victorian tracery. The north aisle is another Victorian addition, with a complementing curvilinear east window.

Outside stands an old cross head on a modern shaft, and there is a good selection of 18th-century table tombs.

Nearby: Eastnor, St John the Baptist

St Michael

A few miles to the north of Ledbury stands the small Norman Church of St Michael. This well-preserved country church contains a great treasure – a Norman font.

St Michael's is a plain two-cell sandstone building. It has been described variously as 'Saxon–Norman' and 'early Norman', but there is no evidence of Saxon stonework present, suggesting that it is indeed the latter. Its stark simplicity gives a surprisingly spacious feel.

At the west end of the nave stands a carved stone font, considered to be one of the finest examples of Romanesque carving in the country,

from the masons of the Herefordshire School of stone carvers. Three crouching figures, pieced together in 1878 support the stem and bowl (below). The stem bears an interlaced single strand pattern, above which the baptism of Christ is depicted, and in which the figure of Christ has an infant face oddly ornamented by a thin moustache. The Trinity is completed by a dove symbolising the Holy Spirit and the hand of God raised in benediction. The carvings include the symbols of the four Evangelists and a pair of facing doves; the stonework is executed with fine fluid artistry.

St Bartholomew Old Church CCT

This is the simplest type of rural early Norman church – unadorned and mostly unchanged – and set in unspoilt Worcestershire countryside.

St Bartholomew's stands next to Church House Farm, a 17th-century black-and-white timbered farmhouse perched in a field above the Sapey Brook. Recent excavations have also revealed evidence of an earlier church here.

Of basic two-cell construction, the church managed to survive being used as a farm outbuilding, and has recently been restored thanks to the endeavours of local people. The fittings have gone – they were mostly removed to the new Victorian church – but the little west gallery remains, as do some traces of wall painting, mostly 17th century, on the north wall. The floor is clay and gravel, and the Norman arched doorway shelters within a fine weathered oak porch, which is smothered with honeysuckle in the summer. Simple Early English lancet windows admit some light to the nave and chancel.

Nearby: Pembridge, St Mary the Virgin; Shobdon, St John the Evangelist

MATLOCK BATH
St John the Baptist FoFC

This beautiful little private Arts and Crafts chapel, designed by Sir Edward Guy Dawber, the first President and one of the founders of the Council for the Preservation of Rural England, was built at the behest of Mrs Harris, who lived at The Rocks, in 1897. It was built to commemorate relatives, and stands precariously on a steep slope overlooking the gorge and Artists' Corner (so-called because its spectacular scenery made it a favourite haunt of artists). Among the artists commissioned within the building were Louis Davis, who designed the glass at the east end, and George Bankart, who was responsible for the barrel-vaulted ceiling with its delightful motif of flying birds.

Nearby: Bakewell, All Saints; Hassop, All Saints

PEMBRIDGE
St Mary the Virgin

The most striking feature of this 14th-century church is its free-standing octagonal bell tower, one of seven in Herefordshire. Free-standing towers in the Marcher counties were often defensive in nature, but that is clearly not the case with this Scandinavian-looking stone and wood structure,

although holes in its door are claimed to have been made by musket balls during the English Civil War.

The tower was built, like the church, in the 14th century. Its first stage is stone with a pyramidal stone-tiled roof. This is surmounted by a weather-boarded second stage, also topped by a smaller pyramidal stone-tiled roof. A final weather-boarded stage has a small shingled spire. Inside is a tangle of massive oak timber trusses and rafters, arranged vertically, horizontally and diagonally; these both brace the tower and provide support for the bells. The oldest timbers – four corner posts – have been tree-ring dated to the early part of the 13th century. One interesting sugges-tion for the existence of the bell tower is that the bells were housed in an open temporary framework during the construction of the church and, for lack of resources – as a tower was never built for the church – remained in situ.

The church has a spacious nave and broad aisles, with pleasing three-light Geometrical windows. This style is continued into the transepts: the windows here are elegantly tall and slender. The east window of the chan-cel is an exceptional example of the Geometric style too – more complex and more developed than those in the aisles, but in pleasing visual propor-tion to the chancel arch. The south transept also contains traces of medieval wall painting, and 17th-century murals of the Creed and Lord's Prayer.

The north porch is the most recent part of the church – late 14th century – and has a fine stone ribbed and vaulted ceiling. The door bears an original sanctuary knocker, and inside are recesses in the wall in which an oak beam was placed to reinforce the door in times of danger.

Nearby: Lower Sapey, St Bartholomew Old Church; Shobdon, St John the Evangelist

PETERCHURCH
St Peter

The Church of St Peter is an ancient and fascinating building on the banks of the River Dore in the northern reaches of Herefordshire's Golden Valley. Unusually, its principal architectural features range from the Saxon period to the late 20th century.

The village of Peterchurch is most known for its glorious views of the nearby Black Mountains, and for the spire of St Peter's Church. In the 1940s the original 14th-century spire was found to be unsafe and was reduced in height by two-thirds, leaving a stump that was to be eventually re-built. By the 1970s urgent action was needed, and it was decided to recreate the original tower in fibreglass, complete with a gilded weathercock. Seen from a distance, rising through a low-lying autumnal mist, it is an unmistakeable landmark, much as it would have been in past centuries, but, close to, it is an unwelcome and unnecessary addition to an interesting church.

Saxon stonework from the 9th century is evident in the foundations and lower courses of the walls of St

Peter's, and the semicircular apse is very fine. The church guide says that the stone altar is Saxon too; though this is not substantiated, it is certainly old, and a rare survivor of the Reformation.

One really has to go inside to appreciate St Peter's and look directly down the nave to the apse. The whole building suddenly appears much larger inside than outside. Three arches separate nave from choir, choir from chancel, and the chancel from the apse, ending in a vanishing point of a narrow Norman window. Walking down through each arch, it can be seen that each one is scaled, from the largest, separating the nave and choir, to the smallest apse arch. Whether consciously done or not, it is an effective optical illusion. There is no ready explanation for the need to divide the church into four sections, but one possible reason might be that the original west end of the church may have been where the chancel arch is now, and that the church was extended westwards soon after (although the west end of the nave bears marks of an earlier and much lower roof). Another possible explanation may be that there was an early tower that stood over the present ante-apse chancel. The tower at the west end is later – an Early English addition – and was clearly used in times of danger. The entrance has always been elevated, accessible only by ladder, and the walls are extremely thick.

REPTON
St Wystan

Christianity was first preached on this site in the 7th century. Here the Kings of Mercia were converted, and an abbey founded. In the 8th century a church was built, possibly as a baptistry. It was converted later to a burial place for members of the Mercian royal family and this mausoleum would become one of the most important examples of Anglo Saxon architecture in the country. The early burial chamber (right) was built below ground level and roofed over with wood; the first burial was that of King Aethelbald. King Wiglaf had the crypt altered for his eventual burial: the wooden roof was removed; and columns and pilasters were constructed to support a stone-vaulted roof, above which a new chancel was built,

The carving is unsophisticated compared to that found in Herefordshire, but, nevertheless, has its own naive charm: a crude, chequered pattern encloses a cross, supported by two figures each with their hand on their hip. The jambs are heavily worn: this is said to be as a result of local archers sharpening their arrowheads against the stonework.

Inside is a similarly early Norman font: it has much the same style of carving, with an Agnus Dei, a man's head protruding from the mouth of a beast, a similar beast seeming to eat its own tail, and two very primitive human figures. There are hatchments of the Fitzherbert family and of Lord St Helens, and, carelessly overlapping the north part of the Norman chancel arch, an imposing monument to Francis Fitzherbert and his son John.

In the churchyard there is the plinth of what many believe to have been a Saxon stone cross, and a grave to a victim of the Titanic disaster.

of Elizabeth I. The parish church is relatively unknown but is full of interest.

The church sits on a small rise, opposite Tissington Hall. It is an early Norman building much restored by the Victorians, and offers a wealth of surprises. The first is the tympanum in the relatively modern south porch.

VOWCHURCH
St Bartholomew

St Bartholomew's Church, on the banks of the River Dore, is a modest Norman church built of red sandstone, whose main interest lies in the unusual timber work within.

The Norman part of the church is not significant, but it was extended and modified in the 14th century and the join between Norman and 14th-century walls can easily be seen from outside. Inside, a rectangular space is divided into nave and chancel by a wooden screen. The most striking feature of the interior, however, is the scaffoldlike arrangement of timbers supporting the 17th-century roof. Unusually, all the structural forces here are born by these internal timbers that rest against the walls rather than by the stone walls themselves. Massive oak posts support trusses from which queen posts rise, bracing the gabled roof. The half-timbered bell tower, dating from the early 16th century, is also supported on an internal oak frame.

The screen has some basic but interesting carvings: crude depictions of Adam and Eve decorate the tops of the central arch posts; and, above the central arch, are two dragons' heads. The carver, probably a semi-skilled 17th-century carpenter, is commemorated on a diamond-shaped board. He evidently had trouble working out his spacing: a board on the chancel wall bears the inscription 'VIVE UT POSTEA VIVAS' (which translates as 'live in order to live hereafter') but the last two letters are crammed into an impossibly small space. Below this is a green man, a male head with a leaf trailing from his mouth.

In the large churchyard, part of which is managed as a refuge for wildlife, the older sandstone head-stones have weathered badly. A marble cross marks the grave of the Revd Skeffington Hume Dodgson, younger brother of Charles Dodgson, of *Alice in Wonderland* fame.

Nearby: Abbey Dore, Holy Trinity and St Mary; Kilpeck, St Mary and St David

St Peter and St Paul

Not many churches can claim to have been moved because of a flooding river, but St Peter and St Paul's church was inundated by flooding from the nearby River Wye, and moved back from the river to its present position.

St Peter and St Paul is a 14th-century church dismantled and reconstructed in 1740, after catastrophic flooding of the nearby River Wye about five years earlier. Most of the original stones were used to rebuild the unbuttressed tower, nave and chancel. Inside is the original Norman font, which has possibly been cut into an octagonal shape following damage during the flood. Above the church in a field there is a treefilled hollow containing a sort of mortared wall from which water from an underground spring flows. This is known as St Peter's Well, and is believed locally to be holy.

Although the church is of no particular importance, its setting – still close to the River Wye, with a wooded ridge to the north – is of great charm, and a visit here can be combined with a pleasant riverside walk.

Nearby: Kinnersley, St James

YOULGREAVE (OR YOULGRAVE)
All Saints

This is a large gritstone parish church in a small Peak District village. The church tower is considered to be one of the finest in Derbyshire, while inside there is a wealth of detail – funerary monuments, stone carving and excellent Tudor roof work. However, the most striking feature of All Saints' Church is a stained-glass window, the fruit of a collaboration between two leading Pre-Raphaelite artists.

All Saints', as it stands today, is mostly 14th and 15th century, with remnants of the 12th-century Norman church visible in the wall of the north aisle and in the arcades. The church contains many details of interest. Opposite the south doorway, at the junction of the north aisle and west extension, a most appealing late 12th-century carving of a figure with ruffed collar, scroll and staff is set into the wall. Near the monument to Roger Rooe in the north aisle, is an interesting piscina set on a carved head. Two fine medieval tombs can be seen in the chancel: the 13th-century tomb of Sir John Rossington, who is shown holding a heart in his hands; and a more elaborate 15th-century alabaster tomb to Thomas Cokayne, who is shown wearing armour and

who was killed in a brawl over a marriage settlement. This figure shows an interesting symbolic convention of the time: Cokayne died before his father, and the effigy is considerably

A 12th century carving of a pilgrim

smaller (about three feet long) than if his father had died before him.

The east window in the chancel is most arresting: four William Morris angels are set centrally above a five-light window. The window contains stained glass by Edward Burne-Jones: St Matthew and St Mark are to the left of Christ, and St Luke and St John are to the right. This window is almost better seen on an overcast day, when, in the darkened church, it gently glows with the warmth of its ochres, reds and yellows.

Northern England

This is a region of Celtic saints and missionaries, from lowland Yorkshire and the Lancashire coast to the mountains and lakes of Cumbria and the windswept North York Moors, thence north through Northumberland and the Border country.

With the exception of Ripon Cathedral, these are mostly little churches and chapels, tucked in sheltered folds of moorland, hidden in forests in the Cheviots, or as in the case of St Helen's in Kelloe, in a former coal-mining village, with its fine late 12th-century carved stone cross. Another fine carving, this one Saxon, can be seen in St Peter's Church in Hackness, itself a delightful church in a steep-sided North York Moors river valley. Further north, Biddlestone Chapel at Netherton has a strong claim to being the most remote church featured in the book, buried in forests on the southern slopes of the Cheviots. The pele tower of St Anne's church in Ancroft bears witness to the Border conflicts – a retreat in time of danger, rather than a place to hang bells.

Wainsgate's Baptist Chapel and the Todmorden Unitarian Church served a more industrial north, the landscape of moorland, mill and factory, while the Quakers sought privacy in more secluded chapels like that at Farfield. To the west of the region, the Lakeland landscapes are the setting for churches such as St Bega's, romantically positioned on the lakeside at Bassenthwaite, and in the upper reaches of Wasdale Head is St Olaf's, claiming to be the smallest parish church in England. On the northwest coast St James's Church stands over the town of Whitehaven, its interior an outstanding example of Georgian design, and further south, overlooking Morecambe Bay, is the rugged little cliff-top church of St Peter's, Heysham.

Right in the centre of the region, to the south of Hadrian's Wall, are two very different churches: Holy Cross in Haltwhistle, which has the distinction of being the most centrally situated church in Britain; and, a few miles to the south, the Friends Meeting House at Coanwood, isolated, hidden from view, and undoubtedly the most peaceful place in the region.

List of Churches

Ancroft, St Anne
Bassenthwaite, St Bega
Bywell, St Andrew
Bywell, St Peter
Castlerigg, St John in the Vale
Coanwood, Friends Meeting House
Easby, St Agatha
Farfield, Friends Meeting House
Ford, St Michael & All Angels
Gillamoor, St Aidan
Gosforth, St Mary
Hackness, St Peter
Haltwhistle, Holy Cross Church
Heptonstall, St Thomas à Becket
Heysham, St Peter
Kelloe, St Helen

Kirkdale, St Gregory's Minster
Lastingham, St Mary
Little Salkeld, St Michael & All Angels
Little Town, Newlands Church
Netherton, Biddlestone Chapel
Ribchester, St Wilfrid
Ripon, The Cathedral of St Wilfrid & St Peter
St Bees, St Bee's Priory
Todmorden, Unitarian Church
Wainsgate, The Baptist Chapel
Wasdale Head, St Olaf
Whitby, St Mary
Whitehaven, St James

ANCROFT

FORD

NETHERTON

HALTWHISTLE

BASSENTHWAITE

COANWOOD   BYWELL

ST BEES WHITHAVEN   CASTLE RIGG   LITTLE
                                  SALKELD
        GOS FORTH   LITTLE TOWN

WASDALE

KELLOE

HEYSHAM

EASBY

GILLAMOOR   WHITBY

RIPON

FAIRFIELD   LASTINGHAM

RIBCHESTER   KIRKDALE

HEPTONSTALL
    WAINSGATE
TODMORDEN

ANCROFT
St Anne

Perhaps more of a castle than a church, the gaunt tower of St Anne's was built in the 13th century as a pele tower, a defensive structure designed to offer protection from the border reivers, during the time of Edward I's abortive attempts to subjugate the Scots.

The tower, known as Ancroft Vicar's Pele, blocked the original Norman doorway and follows a classic pattern of pele towers. There are three floors: the ground level was used as a storage area; the second level served as living quarters and kitchen; the third level was used as sleeping quarters; and the roof, typically flat with battlements, was used as a lookout post and platform from which to repel attackers. A spiral staircase from within the church gave access directly to the upper levels.

The church was also extremely heavily restored in the Romanesque style during the 19th century. At the entrance to the churchyard is a stone mounting block, and, to the west of the tower, is an interesting gravestone to several Poor Clare nuns (the sisters of St Clare) who fled the French revolution and found refuge at nearby Haggerston Castle. Several mounds in nearby fields mark the spots where cottages were burned down after the Black Death had swept through the village in the 14th century.

Nearby: Ford, St Michael and All Angels

BASSENTHWAITE
St Bega

A brisk walk downhill through sheep-grazed fields leads to this beautiful little Lakeland church situated on the eastern shore of Bassenthwaite Lake. St Bega's was visited by William and Dorothy Wordsworth, and Alfred Tennyson, who is believed to have set the opening of his epic poem *Morte d'Arthur* here. The church also appears in Melvyn Bragg's epic novel *Credo*, in which he chronicles the story of St Bega.

The setting is impossibly romantic: a lonely church on the lakeside overlooked by Skiddaw Fell to the north, and with southerly views to Grisedale Pike. St Bega's is a simple homely church, pre-Norman in origin. The chancel arch and random courses of large stones in the east and north walls are remnants of the Norse building. The church has a rather pleasant lopsided feel, with a slightly puzzling late-Norman archway in the chancel that opens into a 14th-century chantry chapel and south aisle, endowed by Adam de Bastenthwayt. An interesting memorial to Robert de Highmoor is squeezed into an impossibly narrow space at the west end of the south aisle.

A beautiful 14th-century lead crucifix hangs over the octagonal pulpit on the north side of the chancel arch.

On the opposite side of the chancel arch is set an iron hourglass bracket, presumably for the convenience of the congregation, who could indicate to a long-winded vicar that his time was up. The Victorians restored St Bega's in 1874, respecting the integrity of the older building.

There is a well-loved feeling about St Bega's; well-polished pews and a sense of quiet order pervade the church.

BYWELL
St Andrew CCT

The only evidence of the once-thriving market town of Bywell is a castle, hall, medieval market cross and two churches of Saxon origin, within a minute's walk of each other. The tower

of St Andrew's, whose multicoloured sandstone walls are 15 feet thick, reuses Roman stone; the lower part dates from 850AD with the upper stages added in the 10th and 11th centuries.

The tower may have had a defensive purpose, but the effect of the different-coloured sandstone used in its construction is a visual delight. Set in the top of the tower are simple, well-carved double windows with surrounding moulded dripstones. The tower stands at the west end of a church whose nave and chancel are 13th century; a Victorian restoration enlarged the original church, retaining for the most part the style of tall slender lancet windows throughout and giving a pleasing unity to a church whose structure was built over a period of 1,000 years.

The furnishings of the interior date mostly from the 19th century and

include a fine reredos and good
stained glass by William Wailes, a
Victorian grocer and tea dealer turned
stained-glass designer (who is buried
in nearby St Peter's Church). Both
inside and outside there is a very
interesting selection of grave slabs,
considered to be the best medieval
collection in Tynedale. These are
decorated with symbols of the trades
or professions of those commemorated: shears; a soldier's sword and
shield; and a hunting horn and book.

Nearby: Bywell, St Peter

BYWELL
St Peter

St Peter's Church, like its neighbour
St Andrew's, has a defensive tower,
whose original entrance was halfway
up the tower and only reachable by
ladder. There are grooves in the
stonework by the west door that were
probably made by the sharpening of
arrowheads.

Elements of the church can be
traced to their Saxon origins. Parts of
the nave clearly date from this period,
as do the arched windows in the
north wall, and a 1990s excavation
uncovered extensive Saxon foundations
underneath the tower. The church was
extended by the Normans, who built
the lofty chancel with its three elegant
Early English lancet windows filling
the width of the east end. St Peter's
was severely damaged by fire in 1285,
and, when it was rebuilt shortly after,
the tower and a south aisle were
added, and the nave shortened.

The chantry chapel on the north side, added in the 14th century, contains outstanding examples of window tracery in the reticulated style. In the late 19th century the chancel arch was rebuilt; it is believed to be a faithful reproduction of the original Early English arch.

Outside, on the south aisle wall, there is a rare example of a scratch clock, a type of rudimentary sundial into which is inserted a stick or rod, whose falling shadow can be measured against the scratched marks indicating the times of masses and other services. There are many interesting headstones and tombs in the churchyard too: carved cherubs, serpents, skulls and scythes abound; there are some poignant inscriptions, including the rather rueful 'Life how short! Eternity how long!'; and a headstone to a Christopher Wycliffe: 'for 23 years a faithfull [sic] and honest servant, erected by his grateful mistress Miss Hind'.

Nearby: Bywell, St Andrew

CASTLERIGG
St John's in the Vale

This is a little Lakeland church in surroundings of rugged beauty. Though it is first referred to in the 16th century, most of the church dates from the mid-19th century. It is described as having a small tower and, indeed, the tower more closely resembles a crenellated chimney.

Its most notable feature is a Sir George Gilbert Scott altar, which came from Crosthwaite Church. The most puzzling thing about the church is why it should have been built in this placid and inaccessible valley: the explanation may be that the road which passes the church was once an important route, part of a track leading from Matterdale over the fells to Wanthwaite and thence to the Naddle Valley.

Nearby: Little Town, Newlands Church

COANWOOD
Friends Meeting House HCT

In an out-of-the-way upland valley south of Hadrian's Wall stands one of the oldest remaining Friends Meeting Houses in Northumberland.

Close to a farmhouse in a small tree-shaded enclosure by a stream, this plain, unornamented building is testament to the dignity of simple worship. The building was founded by Cuthbert Wigham in 1760, and was originally roofed in heather thatch; this was replaced in the early 1800s by a Welsh slate roof.

In the interior the aroma of scrubbed pine pervades the air. The room is simplicity itself – a flagstone floored space divided into two sections. The west section contains a set of benches facing a row of two raised elders' benches, while the east section has a fireplace set in the wall. A panelled wooden screen separates the two sections, the inner parts of which can be raised or lowered by a simple pulley mechanism. Presumably this is to conserve heat around the fireplace, as the winter cold here must be extreme. Coanwood is a place of peace and an invitation to all who come here to be quiet and still for a moment or two.

Nearby: Haltwhistle, Holy Cross

GOSFORTH
St Mary

Situated in Cumbria to the west of Wasdale, Gosforth's St Mary's Church has an exceptional collection of Viking stone carving; these have remained constant in a church that has been through successive and radical rebuilding.

There may well have been a church here before the 10th century, a wattle and daub affair whose remains would have disintegrated with the passing of time. St Mary's Church itself started life as a rectangular Norman building,

the only remnants of which – some incised stone mouldings – can be seen in the south wall of the churchyard. This early building was more or less replaced in the 13th century, underwent further alteration in the 14th century, and, in the late 18th century, lost its thatched roof, had its walls heightened, and, almost unbelievably, one of two fine ancient stone crosses was turned into a sundial. In 1820, and again in 1896, further restoration work took place.

It was during this latter restoration that the extent and importance of the ancient stones at St Mary's came to light, almost literally in the case of one Viking hog-back stone, which was revealed in the foundations when the north wall of the nave was dynamited. This is believed to be a memorial to a Viking warrior, a leader of some significance judging by the complexity and detail of the carving. After this discovery, many more stones were found. The most significant was a second fine hog-back stone – this one believed to commemorate a religious figure. These two stones are now in the west end of the north aisle, and the carving on them is of exceptional quality, with fine cross-cut and braided patterning, and indented overlapping triangular scales.

Nearby: Wasdale Head, St Olaf

HACKNESS
St Peter

This is a most romantically situated church in a picturesque and wooded vale through which runs the River Derwent.

St Peter's Church is a fine and well-preserved Saxon–Norman church with Early English improvements. It has been suggested that this was a priory of Whitby Abbey, but, in the absence of other buildings and lacking any documentary evidence, it seems that St Peter's may have been more of a safe haven for monks fleeing the unwanted attentions of marauding Norsemen. Although compact, the church possesses elegance. A fine Norman arcade leads to the south aisle, while an equally pleasing Early

The carved 7th century cross shaft   *Detail from the font cover*

English arcade on the north opens to the north aisle. The chancel arch is generously proportioned, and one of the imposts has a Scandinavian style of intertwined patterning. In the chancel are some fine 15th-century choir stalls w ith carved misericords – these may have come from Whitby Abbey.

A cross shaft, an outstanding example of 7th-century Northumbrian Anglo Saxon carving, stands at the east end of the south aisle. Although very heav-

ily weathered, some exquisite detail has thankfully survived its use as a gatepost, including inscriptions in Latin, Ogham, Norse, Anglo Saxon, runic, and a strange set of runes resembling pine trees – these latter have defied expert attempts at interpretation.

At the opposite end of the aisle is St Peter's other treasure, a beautiful 15th-century font cover, carved in pear wood and decorated with eight 19th-century figures from Oberammergau.

HALTWHISTLE
Holy Cross

Holy Cross Church enjoys the distinction of being England's most central church building; it is at the midpoint of the longest overland latitude line that can be drawn through Britain.

The church is first mentioned in the Charter of Abroath Abbey as being in the gift of the Tyronenses, an offshoot of the Benedictine order whose monks were urged to maintain and develop their artistic and natural skills, and with whom masons, painters and artists all flourished. Holy Cross Church was built in the 13th century by the master builder of Arbroath Abbey. Pevsner describes it as 'a quite exceptionally complete and well preserved Early English parish church, typically north country in proportions and details'. It is indeed unusual to find a church of this size that is true to one period, and also unusual to find a church where the Victorian restoration so carefully respected the original architectural style. Distinctive tall slender lancet windows pierce the walls, and those at the east end have stained glass by Edward Burne-Jones.

Nearby: Coanwood, Friends Meeting House

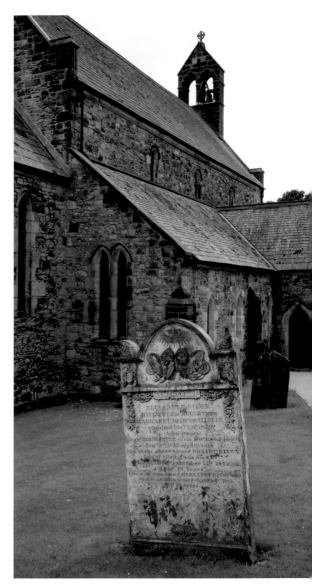

HEPTONSTALL
St Thomas à Becket

It is rare to find two churches occupying the same churchyard. But at Heptonstall the ruins of the 13th-century church of St Thomas à Becket stand side by side with the Victorian Church of St Thomas the Apostle.

The ancient village of Hepstonstall sits on the roof of the Pennines at the top of the northern slopes of the Calder valley. It is no place for those who shrink from fierce winter weather, and the 13th-century church of St Thomas à Becket was built low to withstand the ferocity of the Pennine gales.

The church had a colourful history, at least if local folklore is to be believed: a priest slain at the altar for performing an unlawful wedding ceremony; and mummified cats built into the walls. A severe storm in 1847 demolished the roof, tower and part of the walls, and the villagers, perhaps mindful of John Wesley's description of the old church as the 'ugliest I know' and aware of the difficulties of restructuring such an old building, built a Victorian Gothic church beside it in the same churchyard.

The poet Sylvia Plath is buried in the 'new' churchyard, while in the 'old' part of the churchyard is the grave of the 18th-century coin counterfeiter David Hartley, who was executed in York in 1770.

Nearby: Todmorden, Unitarian Church

HEYSHAM
St Peter

Heysham is one many small villages
that dot the coastline overlooking
Morecambe Bay, and the Church of St
Peter, perched on the side of a cliff,
has a most beautiful setting looking
over the bay to the fells of Cumbria.
St Peter's is a tough little church, built
of rough-hewn stone to withstand the
coastal storms; the masons who extended the church in the 14th and
15th centuries used the same sturdy
type of stone as the earlier builders.

 The site is Saxon, from the 7th or
8th century; the church dates from
just before the conquest. Its Saxon

origins are proclaimed by the remains
of an Anglo Saxon cross close to the
entrance of the churchyard.
Ornamented with foliate scrolled
carvings, there are illustrations of a
swathed figure thought to be Lazarus;
a gabled building; and a seated figure
with a halo. There is an original door
in the west nave wall, now blocked
up. Another Anglo Saxon doorway,
uncovered during the construction
of the north aisle in the late 19th
century, was painstakingly rebuilt
by the incumbent vicar. Inside, near
the south doorway is a splendid

10th-century Viking hog-back tomb. Although not unique in the northwest of England, the one at St Peter's is remarkable for its excellent condition and completeness.

A short walk uphill to the cliff top is the ruin of St Patrick's Chapel, with an intriguing set of stone tombs cut into solid rock.

KELLOE
St Helen

Kelloe is a traditional coal-mining village to the west of Durham; to the east of the village is the site of the long gone medieval village of Church Kelloe. The only remaining building of this bygone settlement is the Norman Church of St Helen. Although the building is kept locked against theft and vandalism, a phonecall will usually elicit a cheery response from the enthusiastic wardens.

The three-stage tower, now supported by a downhill buttress, and the south doorway, somewhat hidden by the later porch, are the most recognisably Norman parts of the church, which comprises nave, chancel and tower. There is also a 14th-century chantry at the northeast end of the nave. Elizabeth Barrett Browning was born nearby at Coxhoe Hall, and was baptised at St Helen's in 1808; the church now hosts a festival in her honour that attracts international interest, and is enthusiastically

supported by the parish.

In 1854, when the chancel was undergoing one of many partial re-buildings, pieces of stone sculpture were uncovered. The quality of the carving was outstanding, and, once pieced together, was found to have been carved by a local sculptor from a single piece of Caen stone in the late 12th century. It is most likely a votive cross to St Helen, mother of Constantine, the first Christian Roman emperor. Moving up from the base, the panels depict: the discovery of the True Cross; Helen and Constantine; and the reclining figure of Constantine under an angel whose hands are raised in benediction. The whole shaft is topped by a cross in circular form, bearing the legend 'IN HOC VINCES' – 'by this conquer'.

The votive cross

as a Romanesque masterpiece. Its form is unique, with aisles, a small nave and apse forming a minute church in its own right. Thickset pillars, with rams' horns carved into the capitals, support a stone-vaulted ceiling, whose arches make a simple pleasing pattern, and, at the east end, a small and deeply splayed arched window admits the only daylight; there is a deep sense of history here.

The interior of the main church, comprising the 11th-century chancel, crossing and aisles, has greatly benefited from London architect John L

Pearson's restoration of 1879: he replaced a plaster ceiling, restoring the groined stone vaulting of the nave and the original barrel vaulting of the chancel, and stripped all the stonework of thick coats of plaster. In doing so, a magnificent, almost Byzantine, space of fine acoustics emerged, one that has become the venue for an increasing number of musical recitals and concerts.

Nearby: Gillamoor, St Aidan; Kirkdale, St Gregory

LITTLE SALKELD, NEAR GLASSONBY
St Michael and All Angels

This is a North Pennines church without a village, since the village was washed away when the River Eden changed its course in the 14th century. The Church of St Michael and All Angels has Norman origins, although a Victorian restoration in 1898 has covered most traces of the earlier church; the most interesting features are to be found in the porch, and outside.

The construction of St Michael's is simple: a low pitch-roofed nave and chancel, and, at the west apex, a stone bellcote for two bells. There are two-light windows in the nave, possibly

Norman, while the chancel is a later addition. The Victorian stained glass is of little interest, but there is a very pleasing modern stained-glass memorial by S M Scott, whose work can also be seen in Hexham Abbey.

Although the church dates back to the Normans, there are remnants here that suggest earlier Saxon use of the site. In the porch is a Viking hog-back tombstone, carved with a triangular tessellating pattern. Beside it are fragments of cross shafts, carved in vivid red sandstone, the same stone as the church, which suggests that they were originally from this site. Their origins are not known, but the curled vinelike carvings are suggestive of Scandinavian work. Outside in the churchyard is a hammerhead Saxon stone cross, also carved from red sandstone.

Nearby: Farfield, Friends Meeting House

LITTLE TOWN
Newlands Church

This little church, whitewashed inside and out, sits snugly behind drystone walls, sheltered by a screen of oak trees near to the watersmeet of Newlands, Scope and Keskadale becks. The valley floor is flat and surrounded by some of the Lake District's gentler fells: Causey Pike and Crag Hill to Cat Bells and High Spy. Newlands Church is, therefore, well worth the tortuous drive through very narrow lanes. The setting certainly impressed the Wordsworths, who discovered it during one of their frequent walks: it makes an appearance in Wordsworth's poem 'To May', a copy of which is displayed in the church.

Beatrix Potter was inspired by this little corner of the Lake District too, and dedicated *The Tale of Mrs Tiggy-Winkle* to the daughter of the vicar of Newlands.

Mr Ingham occupied the pulpit. Undeterred, Hindle gave his sermon from the steps of the pulpit, although one suspects it might not have been without interruption. It was all to no avail however: Hindle was ejected from the parish.

St Peter and St Wilfrid

The cathedral in Ripon is not exactly unnoticeable: the glowing stone of its fine Early English west front dominates the southern edge of the city. But the cathedral has some notable eccentricities, both in its structure and literary associations.

This is the fourth building to stand on this site, replacing a late 11th-century church that was incorporated into the present building in the 12th century, a short-lived Saxon minster from the earlier part of the 11th century, which, in turn, replaced the original 7th-century church of St Wilfrid. The only ancient part of the original church to survive destruction and rebuilding is the Anglo Saxon crypt, which may well have been the first post-Roman stone building to have been constructed in northern England.

The great organ was installed on the pulpitum in 1409, overlooking the choir and chancel; it may have been destroyed during the English Civil War, for another organ was installed in 1695. It was difficult, if not completely impossible, for the organist to see and therefore direct the choir, so a mechanical solution was devised. It is perhaps the quaintest solution in any church in the country: from a low-level slot protrudes a hand, raised as if in cheerful salutation. The hand can be – rather noisily – raised and

lowered to alert the choir. Among the misericords can be seen one that depicts a rabbit being chased down a hole by a griffin, said to have inspired Charles Dodgson (Lewis Carroll), whose father was a residentiary canon of the cathedral, in his writing of *Alice in Wonderland*.

ST BEES, NEAR EGREMONT
St Bees Priory

It took the Normans the best part of 30 years after the invasion to reach this wild coastal area of northwest England. William de Meschines, Lord of Egremont, founded the priory here in 1120 as a subsidiary house to St Mary's Abbey in York. Though commonly thought to be dedicated to St Bega, the main dedication was in fact to St Mary; St Bega has a chapel reserved inside.

When the monks arrived from York, it is probable that they began by occupying an existing church. Rebuilding did not start for another 40 years. The west entrance to the priory is the best-preserved part of the Norman priory, made up of four orders, with highly carved and decorated arches to the first three. In each of the carved orders are sections of alternate red and lighter-coloured soft sandstone. Combined with the effects of penetrating erosion, the entrance is reminiscent of St Magnus's Cathedral in the Orkneys; the outer capitals of the uprights have intricate carving that nature seems to have had a part in, over time forming softer ripples in the carved chevrons. Opposite the west door is a recess containing a stone Celtic cross, with a carved lintel stone – the Dragon Stone – overhead.

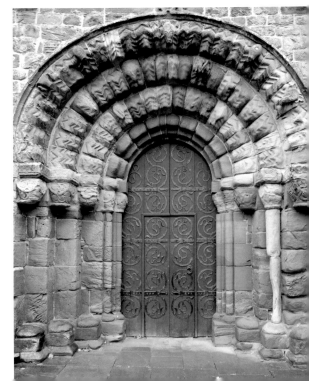

the rock, while on the south wall there is a piscina and main window. Sadly, the interior is disfigured by modern graffiti.

Among the many legends about St Govan and the chapel, the most pervasive was of the curative power of the water, which rose from a natural spring inside the entrance to the hermitage. This was said to have been particularly efficacious for skin complaints, rheumatism and eye diseases, and, in the Middle Ages, the spring was a popular destination for pilgrims. About St Govan himself little of fact is actually known, and it is difficult to discriminate between historical possibility and embroidered nonsense. However, tradition has it that St Govan came to Pembrokeshire from Ireland when he was Abbot of Dairinis, and was forced to take refuge from pirates on the spot where the chapel now stands. A fissure opened in the rock, closing over him until the pirates had gone, then opening up again to allow him out when the coast was clear. Whatever the actual truth of the episode, it seems that St Govan stayed in this spot for the remainder of his life as a hermit in the Celtic monastic tradition of seclusion.

Legend also has it that it is impossible to accurately count the steps leading down to the chapel from the cliff top. This seems to be a legend borne out in practice, as there are several published descriptions that list the steps as respectively 52, 74; and my own count, which was 69.

Nearby: Bosherston, St Michael and All Angels

BOSHERSTON
St Michael and All Angels

My first visit to St Michael's Church was on a sunny, late spring day: the churchyard had just been mown, and the scent of freshly cut grass was in the air. The stonework of this pleasing late-13th-century church, with its characteristic, tall, battlemented tower, shines in the luminous coastal light.

St Michael's was built on the site of an earlier church, and is cruciform in plan. The original Norman windows in the transepts were replaced with simple late-13th-century windows of geometric design, and contain stained glass from the early 20th century. The south porch is a later addition too, dating from the 14th century. The font is Norman, although it has been lined with lead and fitted with an oak lid. In the mid-19th century the church was subject to a Victorian reordering by the first Earl of Cawdor, John Frederick Campbell.

A local schoolmistress had stained glass made for the original squint. It is a depiction of St Nicholas as the patron saint of seafarers, and commemorates the death of her husband during the battle of Jutland. An interesting tomb, thought to be that of the

Dowager Duchess of Buckingham, can be seen in the north transept; her widow's status is symbolised by the carved cloak and veil. In the south transept there is the tomb of a 14th-century crusader.

Outside there is a curious preaching cross. It stands on a double plinth, and its uncharacteristically short upright bears a plain stone cross on which can just be made out the shape of a face. It is possible that the full stone cross was destroyed during the Reformation and that the present cross is a reassembly of surviving pieces.

Nearby: Bosherston, St Govan's Chapel

BRITHDIR
St Mark FoFC

Just a few miles to the east of Dolgellau is the small village of Brithdir, situated high on the southern slopes of the Wnion Valley. It is a place of inspiring mountain views and wooded hillsides. Set back among a tangle of wild rhododendron, azalea, birch and ash and reached by a track bordered by moss-covered boulders, is the Church of St Mark. In this peaceful and

shaded place, the silence is broken only by the song of woodland birds.

St Mark's Church is an unexpected and delightful surprise. Owned and maintained by the Friends of Friendless Churches, it is a rarity in Wales – a listed Grade I Art Nouveau church. It was built at the end of the 19th century as a memorial to the Revd Charles Tooth, chaplain and founder of St Mark's English Church in Florence.

On arrival, one is immediately struck by both the setting of St Mark's and the confidence of its architecture. A walk around the outside reveals an almost organic feel to the building, especially in the lower courses of the east end: it is as if the church has grown from the earth. This was the original intention of the architect Henry Wilson, who asked that all the stonework be unworked. The rest of the stonework is, however, tooled, suggesting that the builders were neither sympathetic to nor comfortable with the notion of rough stonework.

There is a characteristic Arts and Crafts cat-slide roof swooping down to the porch, and highly detailed Art Nouveau window leading.

On entering the church, one moves from the soft greens and greys of the Welsh landscape to a southern European scene: earthy reds and vivid blues give one the sense of being in a Mediterranean village. All is suffused with a warm glow, further enhanced by the materials used in the facings for the pulpit and altar, both beautifully and intricately designed and made by Henry Wilson in typical Arts and Crafts style. The decorated lead font at the west end, also designed by the architect, was made by the Central School of Art in London. The choir stalls are charmingly decorated with a whimsical miscellany of creatures – squirrels and rabbits abound, sharing space with an owl, a kingfisher and a dolphin. The north door is of note too, with its polished walnut panels inlaid with mother of pearl.

CAPEL-Y-FFIN
St Mary

Although the remote church of St Mary at Capel-y-Ffin is set in a sheltering circle of ancient yew trees, it is sometimes inaccessible in the winter if there is heavy snow. The church stands at a bend in the winding road that leads up from the Honddu Valley, goes over the Black Mountains and descends to Hay-on-Wye.

St Mary's church is the chapel of ease to the church of St Eigen, in nearby Llanigon. It is among the smallest chapels of ease in Wales, measuring some 30 feet by 14 feet, and is built of rubble masonry, with dressed door and window jambs; the exterior is whitewashed and the building is topped by a jaunty and extremely lop-sided bellcote holding two medieval bells (one recast in the 19th century). The church is actually orientated southwest to northeast, so the altar is placed at the 'ecclesiastical' east end.

St Mary's was built in 1762, replacing an earlier chapel of which no trace remains, although there are gravestones in the churchyard that date from earlier in the 18th century,

and the base of a stone medieval cross set into a boulder. Also in the graveyard is a simple, elegant inscription in memory of the cartographer David Pelham Bickmore.

Inside, the church is of simple single-cell configuration, with a stone-flagged floor and whitewashed plastered walls. Sturdy chamfered posts support a late-18th-century gallery. The atmosphere inside is dignified and peaceful: a small harmonium, an octagonal wooden pulpit and oak settles are the only furnishings, with stone slab benches against the walls, and a plain altar on which rests a simple cross. There is also a medieval font, which may have come from the earlier church.

Nearby: Cwmyoy, St Martin

St Cadoc

In a remote river valley on the Gower peninsular stands an imposing 14th-century church, dedicated to St Cadoc. It is thought by some to have replaced an earlier church at nearby Llandimore when the latter was encroached upon by the sea; this is conjecture, however. Surprisingly little is known of the history of this splendid church; it is possible that Cheriton was the original settlement of Llandimore, and it is also possible that St Cadoc's was granted to the Order of the Knights Hospitallers, for whom nearby Glebe House, the oldest inhabited house on Gower, was built. Whatever its origins, St Cadoc's is a very fine transitional church, and, as a result of its impressive size, has acquired the anecdotal title of the 'Cathedral of Gower'.

Tales of St Cadoc make him out to be rather formidable: the son of a robber chieftain, the saint is reputed to have pursued, together with his monks, a band of raiders who had sacked his church; having subdued the miscreants by cutting off their hair while they slept, St Cadoc then enticed them into a marsh where they all drowned. Other, more fortunate, would-be raiders were charmed by music into leaving St Cadoc and his followers alone.

The southern porch of St Cadoc's church contains a good example of a decorated doorway: the interior is much restored, with Victorian choir stalls, altar rail, altar and wooden ceiling being hand carved by the Revd J D Davies in 1874. In the chancel arch one can still see the entrance to the rood loft.

Those interested in the life of Sigmund Freud may like to know that his official biographer Ernest Jones is buried in the churchyard, itself a charming and peaceful place lulled by the passing of a nearby stream.

St Melangell

The beautiful, semi-wilderness setting of St Melangell's Church is itself enough to inspire a visit, but within the church are equally compelling reasons to explore further. St Melangell's is situated near the head of Cwm Pennant, in a glaciated landscape at the heart of the Berwyn mountains. Surrounded

by mountains with rough pasture and moorland, this once-wooded valley is now grazed by cattle and sheep; only a handful of dwellings and farms remain as reminders of a once-thriving agricultural community. Elsewhere, the overgrown spoil tips of lead mining and slate and granite quarrying tell of a more industrial aspect to Cwm Pennant's past.

Now no longer serving a parish, St Melangell's has resumed its position as a 'pilgrims" church, for St Melangell's contains the only known Romanesque saint's shrine in Britain, and has been a destination for pilgrims for over one thousand years. In common with most Celtic saints, little is known of St Melangell, but a late 15th-century document, the Historia Divae Monacellae, tells of Monacella or Melangell, the daughter of an Irish king who fled to avoid a forced marriage, and took up a contemplative religious life in Wales. One day a Welsh prince, Brochwel Ysgithrog, was hunting in Pennant; his hounds, pursuing hares into a thicket, found Melangell at prayer, with the hares sheltering under the hem of her cloak. The prince, being moved by her story, gave her the valley for sanctuary, and there she founded a nunnery. After her death she continued to be venerated, and is known as the patron saint of hares.

The shrine of St Melangell

The first impression of St Melangell's is of a simple, substantial, Norman church; this is deceptive. Excavations have revealed evidence of a semi-circular 12th-century apse, replaced in the 18th century by a square stone structure, which was used first as a schoolroom and later as a vestry. Demolition of this stone structure revealed a rounded 12th-century arch; this was carefully restored, giving access to a 'new' apse. In the course of the restoration, the architect Robert Heaton undertook the reconstruction of the saint's shrine, demolished in the 16th century. Great care was used to differentiate between modern and

churches, although this one is unusually graceful and slender, with bells
dating from the 15th and 16th centuries. The nave has unusual, pointed,
barrel-vaulting, and there is a good
Norman font.

LLANBADRIG
St Patrick

The Church of St Patrick, on the north
coast of Anglesey, overlooks the Irish
Sea, in the shelter of a small hillock to
the south, which has the added benefit of shielding a rather less-inspiring
view of the local power-generating
station. It has recently been fully restored
to its original state following vandalism resulting in a catastrophic fire.

The name of the local village –
Llanbadrig – means 'Church of St
Patrick'. There was a church here in
the 5th century, dedicated to St
Patrick, whom local legend has it was
shipwrecked on a nearby island, then
subsequently found his way to
Anglesey, to a cave some way below
the church. He is said to have founded
the original church as thanks for his
safe deliverance. The church fabric
one sees today is 15th century, a
single-cell building divided into nave
and chancel by a transitional arch that
may have been incorporated from an
earlier 13th-century church. Inside
there is a Norman font, possibly from
the earlier church too. The exterior is

plain: solid stone and a tight weather-
proof slate roof tell of wild winter
storms sweeping in from the Irish Sea.

Uniquely, however, the church
combines traditional Christian
features with elements of Islamic
decoration, particularly in the stained
glass and ceramic tiles. Wishing to
make good earlier crude restorations,
the 3rd Lord Stanley of Alderly
(1827–1903), a supporter of Welsh
churches, convert to Islam and the
first ever Muslim Member of
Parliament, offered to provide
restoration funds on condition that
various elements within the church
would also reflect the Islamic
decorative tradition. The resulting

stained glass is a beautiful, geometric non-figurative patterning in blue, white and red, a theme further echoed in the blue tiling of the chancel, and the blue stained glass in the chancel window. There are regular Sunday services at the church.

Nearby: Llaneilian, St Eilian

LLANBEULAN
St Peulan FoFC

The Church of St Peulan is reached by a raised causeway separating two fields, suggesting perhaps that, at one time, the land hereabouts might have been either marshland, or subject to regular flooding. The landscape is rather bare, with the horizon punctu-ated by ugly electricity pylons, but there is something rather inviting about this little church when viewed from the far end of the causeway.

Although the present building is medieval, it is believed to occupy the site of a much earlier 7th-century

church. A plain Norman arch separates the nave from the chancel, while a Transitional arch leads to a south transeptual chapel. The workmanship of the church is rough and ready, yet St Peulan's has an appealing simplicity, and remains generally true to its original form.

The outstanding feature at St Peulan's is a font that is large enough to completely accommodate a young child. There is a crude but powerful Celtic cross carved on the east side, and the north side is decorated with a depiction of a Romanesque arcade. At first thought to be from the 12th century, this font is now believed to date from pre-Norman times, and may have started out life as an altar. If so, contends the historian and writer Peter Lord in *Medieval Vision: The Visual Culture of Wales*, 'as an altar of the pre-Norman period it is a unique survivor in Wales, and, indeed, in Britain'.

Nearby: Tal-y-llyn, St Mary

LLANDELOY
St Eloi FoFC

This gem of an Arts and Crafts-influenced church is tucked away in a field behind the Pembrokeshire village of Llandeloy, overlooking a broad panorama of windswept fields. If it was not for the two bay stone bellcote, one could be forgiven for thinking that here was a long stone barn, albeit in immaculate condition. Outside, parts of the churchyard can get overgrown, and care should be taken to avoid an inadvertent immersion in the 'holy well'.

Designed by the architect John Coates Carter, who also designed the Italianate Caldey Abbey, the church was revived from medieval ruins, using local stone and in a style of small-church architecture ubiquitous throughout Wales. But it is the interior of St Eloi's that makes it so special. A basic two-cell structure, the interior proclaims a pre-Reformation warmth. The nave is separated from the chancel by a glorious rood loft: the altar, and gesso- and tempera-painted reredos are flooded with light from slender and deeply splayed north and south windows.

The impression is one of an interior informed by an intuitive understanding of light and shade. With the north door closed, the nave is quite dark, except for a pool of golden light that

The font at the west end

spills over the font from a high window at the west end. Similarly, a rough stone archway leads to a small chapel on the south side of the nave, into which light falls from a pair of tall lancet windows. The piscina is carved from grey slate.

In abrupt contrast, the nave is furnished with the simplest of benches with an octagonal medieval font at the west end. St Eloi's exemplifies design, material, light, shade and spiritual purpose in a way that exemplifies a synthesis of artistic intuition and detailed forethought.

LLANEILIAN
St Eilian

A wander through leafy lanes to the northeast of Amlwch Port brings one to the Church of St Eilian, a Grade I-listed building. The initial view of this unusual and charming church is of a square, three-stage limewashed tower, surmounted by a 'Rhenish' pyramidical roof. St Eilian's was probably built on the site of an earlier 6th century 'clas'. A glimpse of the elaborately crenellated parapets surmounting the west end of the nave suggests that there has been wealth here, possibly from the offerings of pilgrims who came to visit the Holy Well of St Eilian, closer to the seashore.

The tower is 12th century, while the pleasantly proportioned nave and chancel date from the 15th and 16th centuries respectively. Diagonal buttresses support the four corners of the

nave. One oddity here is the chapel to the southeast – known as St Eilian's Chapel. It is a separate structure, set diagonally to the chancel, with which it is linked by a passageway. The stone chapel is dated to the 14th century, pre-dating the chancel and nave: chapels of this type are indicative of monastic origins, and it may be that this is the site of St Eilian's cell. One can only speculate on the nature of the earlier main body of the church.

Inside, the first impression is of gleaming brass and polished wood, but dominating all are the rood screen and loft. This finely carved oak screen, with intricate foliate patterning, bears in the centre a remarkable painted figure of a skeleton wielding a scythe, on the blade of which is written 'COLYN ANGAUYW PECHOD' (The sting of

death is sin). The date of this striking painting (above) is not certain, but it is likely that it is 16th century. The screen and painting are such arresting features of St Eilian's that it is possible to miss many of the other smaller, but nevertheless intriguing, features that abound: four carved figures of musicians in the chancel roof; a pair of dog tongs, dating from 1748 and used to hold and eject stray dogs from the church; the rare 15th-century, portable wooden altar in the chapel; and a set of pan pipes and clarinet, believed to have been used in the church before the installation of the organ.

Outside there is the stump of a preaching cross, and, as a reminder of the maritime past of Anglesey, numerous grave slabs to seafarers.

Nearby: Llanbadrig, St Patrick

LLANELIEU
St Ellyw FoFC

This remote little 13th-century church, whose irregularly shaped churchyard is now effectively a meadow, is in the foothills of the Brecon Beacons. It can be reached by a winding lane leading from nearby Talgarth, passing the parish church of St Gwendoline. Nearby is Llanelieu Court, which incorporates small fragments of medieval stonework in its fabric; the house is thought to have had monastic affiliation in the 14th or 15th century, and to have been associated with the church of St Ellyw.

Inside, once one has heaved open the exceptionally heavy and, unusually, right-hand-hinged wooden door, a simple but imposing 14th-century rood screen and loft painted in a faded deep red dominate all. Small quatrefoil openings permit a view from the loft to the altar, which is separated from the main body of the church by 17th-century plain wooden rails. Early 20th-century roof repairs led to the obliteration of wall paintings and significant detailing of the screen, but, for the most part, this little church has escaped heavy-handed restoration, particularly during the Victorian era. On the west wall there

are the fragmentary remains of a wall painting of the Tree of Life, and the flagged stone floor shows considerable reuse of grave slabs. On the walls can be seen a series of memorials to the Davies family.

Music recitals are held in the church: a delightful if chilly venue for candlelit music.

Nearby: Talgarth, St Gwendoline

LLANFAGLAN
St Baglan FoFC

St Baglan's Church can be found some two miles south of Caernarfon. Its charm lies principally in its wild and isolated setting; it is a solitary building in the middle of a field overlooking the southern extremity of the Menai Strait, which separates the mainland from the Isle of Anglesey

Encircled by rough dry-stone walling, St Baglan's Church is a simple structure, dating in its present form from the 13th century. The nave is surmounted by a plain stone bellcote; there is a south transeptual addition and a deep porch to the north. This porch is well worth a close look as it incorporates, on the top of the eastern wall, a carved stone from the 5th or 6th century. The inner lintel of the porch doorway is formed by a similar stone.

Inside, the 18th-century social order is clearly illustrated by the mixture of open-backed pews and grander box pews, some of which bear the signatures and dates of the wealthier members of the congregation.

O·YE MOUNTAINS·&·HILLS · BLESS·YE·THE·LORD
PRAISE·HIM·&·MAGNIFY·HIM·FOR·EVER

LLANFAIR KILGEDDIN
St Mary the Virgin FoFC

The Church of St Mary the Virgin is situated in Monmouthshire farmland in the Usk Valley. It is tucked away in a patchwork of fields, off a small country lane by the village of Llanfair Kilgeddin, close to the River Usk and is a quiet place where the only sounds are the occasional squawk of a startled pheasant or the rumble of a nearby tractor.

Like many churches, St Mary's is a later church on an earlier site: the font is Norman, and the chancel screen is from the 15th century. In the north chancel window there are some fragments of medieval glass.

Major rebuilding work took place in the late 19th century, and it is as a result of that work that St Mary's has acquired a unique feature – the sgraffito panels that decorate the nave. The rector at the time was Revd W J

Coussmaker Lindsay, a well-connected gentleman related to Sir Coutts Lindsay, founder of the Grosvenor Gallery (a gathering place for artists such as John Dando Sedding, Edward Burne-Jones, and Heywood Sumner).

The Revd Lindsay's wife Rosamund died unexpectedly in 1885. Her husband, together with John Sedding, who was already working on the restoration of St Mary's, reusing as much of the original material as was possible, asked Heywood Sumner if he would undertake a decoration of the interior of St Mary's as a memorial to his wife. Heywood Sumner devised a decorative scheme of 16 panels for the church using the sgraffito technique. This process, which can be traced back to the Romans, uses several differently coloured overlays of thin plaster, each of which can be scratched through to reveal the colour underneath. The panels were based on the morning psalm 'The Benedicite',

which, with its references to nature, was popular with Arts and Crafts artists. At Llanfair, Sumner turned to the Usk Valley, the nearby church of Llanvihangel Gobion and the Sugar Loaf mountain for inspiration. The results at St Mary's are a series of illustrations in which clouds, mountains, trees, fields, the ploughman, grazing sheep, the birds in the air, running water and human figures are reduced to a elegant and moving simplicity. The effect is extraordinary: a building that in the decorative sense has merged with the landscape in which it stands.

In the 1980s the church was declared redundant and was passed to the Friends of Friendless Churches who undertook its restoration with a major grant from CADW and the Pilgrim Trust. John Morgan-Guy, of the FOFC, describes the decorative memorial scheme as '…one of the great Biblically-inspired artworks of Wales'.

LLANFECHELL
St Mechell

Not many churches have the benefit of a personal journal documenting much of daily church life but, among the 18th-century parishioners of the Church of St Mechell, in the north of

Anglesey, was one William Bulkeley of Brynddu, a diarist and squire. His diaries chronicled social habits and customs, church administration, his own family matters, and local life. He

was a man of mischievous wit and acerbic humour who has provided us with an informative and highly personal account of parish life at Llanfechell. A distant relation of Bulkeley was appointed rector, but a September entry remarks, 'Onely [sic] a piece of sermon 14 minutes long, he promised the other piece a fortnight hence, thus it has been always used by this man to make one sermon serve for a month.'

pews and the introduction of electric lighting. There are continuous stone benches around the nave dating from the 12th century, the floor is of lime ash, and there is fine 15th-century arch-bracing to the nave roof. Services are still held here, using candles and oil lamps for lighting, and there is no heating. Burials are still held in the churchyard.

Nearby: Llantwit Major, St Illtud

LLANGADWALADR
St Cadwaladr

This small but surprisingly ornate church in the southeast of Anglesey was originally called Eglwys Ael, Welsh for 'Wattle Church'. This refers to the early 5th-century church established as a Royal monastery by the Kings of Gwynedd from nearby Aberffraw. And, until 1920, the tradition of a Royal appointment of the priest (and latterly rector) at the

church was maintained.

The principal features of interest are a memorial stone set in the church wall to King Cadfan of Gwynedd. In translation it reads 'KING CADFAN, THE WISEST AND MOST RENOWNED OF ALL KINGS'. His grandson, King Calwaladr, was the last British King to maintain a semblance of unity among the various British kingdoms and tribes as they collapsed in the face of the Anglo Saxon push westwards. It is believed that Calwaladr became a monk at the monastery of Eglwys Ael, and that, on his death during a pilgrimage to Rome in 682 AD, his body was brought back and buried here. The church certainly took its name from that time.

Two notable Anglesey families have helped shape the church: the Owens and the Meyricks. The stained-glass east window celebrates the return of Owain ap Llywelyn from the Battle of Bosworth, and the north and south side chapels were added in the 17th century by Richard Meyrick – a descendant of the Owens – and Colonel Hugh Owen.

Nearby: Llangefni, St Cwyfan

LLANGEFNI
St Cwyfan

The Church of St Cwyfan is on a rocky islet connected to the mainland of Anglesey by a tidal causeway. It is a setting of breathtaking beauty and remoteness, much appreciated by those who come across the church, although, in *A Topographical Dictionary of Wales*, 1833, Samuel Lewis wrote: '…the whole aspect of the place is dreary and desolate. The surrounding scenery is not enlivened either by variety or beauty, and the only views which possess any interest are those extending over the bay.'

The church dates from the early 13th century, and may have been a replacement for an earlier building. In the 14th and 15th centuries a north aisle was added; the blocked arcade on the north side can still be clearly made out.

The broad bay, walled by cliffs to the north, was at one time a modest coastal port and it appears from maps of the 1700s that the church was per-manently connected to the mainland. But, by the time that Lewis wrote his entry, erosion and the Black Death had

taken their toll, decimating the local population and leading to the virtual disappearance of the mainland village. The causeway had become tidal, and the islet was eroding fast too. Graves were toppling into the sea, and eventually the entire north aisle was claimed. St Cwyfan's Church was superseded in 1871 by a new church on the mainland, and, by 1893, the original church's roof had gone and it was in a state of complete neglect. It was left to the farsightedness of architect and archaeologist Harold Hughes to undertake restoration, a major part of which was the construction of a solid sea wall around the islet to prevent further erosion by the sea. At the time of writing, CADW is sponsoring original limewash on the exterior of the church, and the church is the subject of an extensive archaeological and historical investigation by a university team.

One can only access St Cwyfan's at low tide, when the original causeway is accessible, but the church is opened regularly through the summer months, and there is still an occasional service held. Although the nearest town is Llangefni, it is far easier to access the bay from Aberffraw.

Nearby: Llangadwaladr, St Cadwaladr

LLANRHAEADR
St Dyfnog

This is a quiet place, in part thanks to a new road that has taken traffic away from the village. St Dyfnog is thought to have chosen this site in the 6th century because of the well: the village name, Llanrhaeadr, means church (llan) and cascade or waterfall (rhaeadr). And the well can still be found by taking a short walk into the woods to the south.

The church building is a typical no-nonsense Welsh church, with a thick-set 13th-century tower, while the main body of the church is an equally proportioned double nave, dating from the 1400s. This configuration is known in Welsh as an 'eglwys ddwbl' (a double-aisled church), and occurs frequently throughout this part of Wales. The church shows signs of wealth that contradict its rural position: the double nave, the excellent carved timber porch, the fine detailed carvings on the panelled and barrel-vaulted oak ceilings within and most notably an outstanding 16th-century Jesse window that floods the north aisle with gently muted colours. These signs of apparent wealthy endowment may well have resulted from the offerings left by pilgrims at the well, which the saint, through his habit of

doing penance by immersion in the icy torrent, had imbued with the power to heal 'scabs and the itch' as well as – according to some – smallpox, deafness and dumbness. Such was its fame that it was still being visited in the 18th century.

The Jesse tree stained glass is indeed magnificent: it bears the date 1533, and tells the story of the ancestry of Christ through the House of David. The window that today's visitor sees is much as it would have been when the window was first set at the east end of the nave. And if the window itself is extraordinary, then so is the story of its survival. To protect it from marauding Parliamentarian troops, the glass was dismantled and buried in an oak chest either in the churchyard, or more likely in the nearby woods. At the Restoration the glass was reinstated, costing £60.

There is earlier stained glass too: at the west end of the church is a window containing 15th-century glass, found lying in a heap in a nearby cottage about 120 years ago. It is heavily fragmented, and may be the remnants of a window – or windows – destroyed during the English Civil War.

The 16th century stained glass 'Jesse Tree'

Take a moment to look at the porch in more detail: it bears fine carving and is thought to have incorporated the rood screen from the church.

Look too at the superb carved angels on the corbels under the vaulted and panelled roof. John Betjeman had a criterion for visiting a church – is it worth cycling several miles against a headwind to see? Emphatically 'yes'.

LLANRHAEADR-YM-MOCHNANT
St Dogfan

St Dogfan's Church is where William Morgan, vicar from 1578 to 1588, completed his translation of the Bible into Welsh. St Dogfan's also stands on the site of a much earlier 'clas'.

St Dogfan's is a mixture of periods and styles: the tower base seems to be the earliest – possibly 9th century – with the upper part of the tower being rebuilt in the 17th and 18th centuries; the nave dates from the 13th century. The chancel, sanctuary and side chapels were added in the 1500s. The Georgian pulpit is believed to incorporate two panels from William Morgan's original pulpit. The ceiling over the chancel is of interest with its oak barrel-vaulting supported on arched beams and well-carved bosses.

One of the principal curiosities of St Dogfan's is the Cwgan Stone, a rather battered 9th-century tomb slab discovered embedded in the church fabric in the 1850s. It is carved with a Celtic cross, and bears the inscription 'CORGOM FILIUS EDELSTAN' (Cwgan, son of Edelstan).

Nearby: Cwm Pennant, St Melangell

The 9th century Cwgan stone

LLANTWIT MAJOR
St Illtud

John Wesley's journal comments, apropos the Church of St Illtud at Lllantwit Major, 'I suppose it has been abundantly the most beautiful as well as the most spacious church [in] Wales.' St Illtud's is also a curious church, not least because the building comprises both an original Norman west church, built near the site of an earlier Celtic church, and a 13th-century east church, built for monastic use. The original Celtic monastery of St Illtud, a major centre of Christianity from about 500 AD is thought to have been just to the north of the existing west and east churches

and it has been claimed to be Britain's oldest centre of learning. As with most Celtic monastic foundations, it was a series of wooden buildings, and the only known remains from this period are a collection of carved stones, now housed in the west church.

The present church is formed of three buildings: the now-ruined Galilee Chapel to the extreme west, formed of a crypt and chapel above, latterly endowed as a chantry by Sir Hugh Raglan in the 15th century; the west church, 11th century in origin, of cruciform shape, and rebuilt in the 15th century; and the east church,

built in the 13th century for the
Benedictine monks of Tewkesbury
Abbey in Gloucestershire. The result is
a building of great interest and varia-
tion, strung out along a rambling
west–east axis.

The east church overlapped the west
church, taking in the original tower.
The transepts were demolished, and a
nave was constructed, with a north
and south aisle. Interesting features of
the south aisle are the internal flying
buttresses, which were installed at the
beginning of the 20th century to
counter the outward thrust that had
resulted from the raising of the roof
(and associated higher walls). Inside,
the plain nave and aisles, with square
columns and simple Early English
arches, contrast vividly with the ornate
stone reredos, whose 22 niches stand
empty and bereft of their original
carved saints and apostles. Curvilinear,
Early English and Perpendicular styles
are represented in the windows, while
a contemporary carved wooden Crucifixion rood straddles a 15th-century
painted rood background. There are
two wall paintings of great interest
here: one, on the north nave wall, shows
St Christopher, while on the north
wall of the chancel is an exquisite
simple depiction of Mary Magdalene.

In the west church there is a good
collection of stone effigies and the
Celtic Stones. These latter date from
the 9th and 10th centuries: the Houelt
Stone commemorates Hywel ap Rhys,
King of Glywysing; and the St Illtud
or Samson Cross is dedicated for the
soul of St Illtud by Abbot Samson. Of
the two stone effigies, the monk is the
most interesting, being a coped stone
whose upper surfaces bear pleasing
carved stone patterns, surmounted by
the tonsured head of a monk.

St Illtud's is an exceptionally interesting church to visit, not withstanding an ugly glazed screen at the base
of the tower that interrupts an otherwise fine view down the length of the
whole building.

_____

Nearby: Llanfrynach, St Brynach

The Samson cross

MOLD

St Mary the Virgin

———

The Church of St Mary the Virgin occupies a prominent position on a rise overlooking the market town of Mold. It is an imposing building of heavily weathered Cefn sandstone, and is a fine example of Perpendicular

architecture; the interior conveys a tremendous sense of space and light, and the whole church is redolent of its Tudor patron, Margaret Beaufort, Countess of Richmond and her husband Lord Thomas Stanley, Lord of the manor of Mold.

St Mary's comprises a long spacious nave, with a north and south aisle, above whose arches run string courses of carved stone animals – elephants, unicorns and bears among them: it is a feature that is continued on the outside of the church too. At the east end is an apsidal chancel. Due to monetary constraints, the clerestories are not as high as was first planned; the chancel arch too, a very grand affair, remained blocked up for the same reasons. It was only when Sir George Gilbert Scott, the great Victorian master of Gothic Revival, undertook a major restoration of St Mary's, that the chancel arch was opened up and an apsidal chancel added. Scott also replaced the rather poor central nave roof with one

that matched the splendours of the original 15th-century north aisle roof. Everywhere there are reminders of the patronage of the church by the Stanley family, whose coats of arms are to be seen in the nave being borne by angels placed between the springs of the arches.

The stained glass is mostly good Victorian, particularly in the apse windows. There are two fine examples of stained glass work by Clayton and Bell: a five-light window in the south aisle at the east end; and, further west, a depiction of Christ's discourse on the last judgement, taken from Matthew. Next to this is a pre-Raphaelite window by Alexander Booker.

The key, in the event of the church being locked, is available from a cheerful lady in the nearby electronics shop.

NEVERN
St Brynach

In the churchyard of St Brynach's, in the picturesque Pembrokeshire village of Nevern, stands a Celtic cross, considered to be one of the best examples

of its kind in Wales. The village and church, all part of the original Norman settlement, huddle comfortably in the valley of the River Nyfer –

The Celtic cross, St Brynach

a timeless rural setting.

Built on the site of St Brynach's 6th-century 'clas', the crenellated tower is the only surviving Norman part of the church; the nave, chancel and short transepts are Perpendicular, dating from the 15th and 16th centuries. Most striking among the items of interest at St Brynach's are the various inscribed and carved stones to be found in and around the church. Embedded in the window sills of the north transept are two stone slabs: the first, known as the Maglocunus Stone, bears inscriptions in Latin and ogham script to 'MAGLOCUNUS, SON OF CLUTORIUS', and is believed to date from the 5th century; the second, the Cross Stone, is probably part of an 8th- or 9th-century grave slab, and is carved with an elegant, corded cross-shaped design.

Outside, to the east of the porch is the Vitalianus Stone, also inscribed in Latin and ogham, while on the north side of the church, in the west corner of the second chancel window there is a stone fragment with indistinct Latin lettering believed to be a remnant from the latter days of Roman occupation. But the dominant stone of interest is also to the east of the porch – the Celtic Cross. This fine piece of carving stands some 13 feet high, and is carved with graceful interlaced patterns, set into a series of panels on each face of the upright, on top of which is set a carved cross. There are other stones of great antiquity here and nearby, and such variety of antiquities justifies an extended visit.

Nearby: Bayvil, St Andrew

PATRICIO
St Issui

Part of the pleasure of visiting the Church of St Issui is in finding it. St Issui's looks east over the Grwyne Fawr valley and can only be reached by a careful drive (or an arduous walk) along narrow, steep twisting country lanes leading up from either Crickhowell, or from Stanton (turning off the lane that leads to Llanthony Abbey).

St Issui's is a simple two-cell church with 11th-century origins. Built on a made-up mound, it has suffered from unstable foundations. In 1928 it was found that the south wall had spread substantially off the vertical, pulling the roof with it. Timely intervention saw the roof jacked up, the wall underpinned and the roof reset. Evidence suggests that a similar, but more catastrophic movement, took place in the 13th century.

On entering the church, one's attention is immediately drawn to the rood screen and loft. Although the carved figures have long gone, it is an exceptional piece of craftsmanship, made from Irish oak in the 15th century, and bearing intricate foliate patterning. Unlike many rood screens, the one at St Issui's was never painted, and consequently has an unblemished appearance. On the west wall of the nave is a fascinating, if somewhat faded wall painting of Time – a skeleton with scythe, hourglass and spade – reminding us of our brief sojourn in this world. In fact there are a number of wall paintings in the nave, fragments of which peep out from behind the religious texts that James I commanded should obscure all such 'Popish' frivolity. There is an interesting circular Norman font at the west end too, and St Issui's has no less than three stone altars, all of which escaped the reformers' zeal during the reign of Elizabeth I.

Outside, a short walk leads steeply down to a wooded dell through which runs a vigorous stream. This is the place of the Holy Well, whose approach is marked by a pilgrim stone bearing an inscribed cross. It is a place of peace and quiet, ideal in which to imagine the saint living in his nearby cell or to recall his murder there by a disgruntled traveller.

Nearby: Cwmyoy, St Martin

RUTHIN
Rug Chapel *CADW*

This diminutive 17th-century chapel in its garden setting is one of Denbighshire's treasures. Though of no great merit from the outside, the interior is a riot of carving and decoration.

Rug Chapel was commissioned in the mid-17th century by Colonel 'Old Blue Stockings' William Salesbury, Royalist Governor of Denbigh Castle during the English Civil War. Almost no surface has escaped the attention of the artists and craftsmen: intricate carvings ripple over beams and panels; painted angels smile enigmatically down from the corbels; while a panoply of beasts, imaginary and real, ornament the roof in a seemingly endless frieze. The roof is extraordinary, with its massive timber braces, beams and inset panels all painted with entwined rose motifs. The same must be said for the gallery, which makes an ideal point from which to admire the roof, and to look at the chandelier in the centre of the chapel, from which cherubs dangle in cheerful abandon. The colours are said to be more or less true to the originals. One

is brought back to notions of mortality however by a macabre wall painting of a recumbent skeleton, with the legend 'UT HORA SIC VITA', colloquially translated as 'life is very short'. And at ground level, there are fabulous beasts carved into the monolithic bench ends, and yet more carving on the family pews.

Rug Chapel has a powerful effect on all who visit; even the architect Sir Edwin Lutyens wrote of its influence on his own work, particularly in relation to his magnum opus the Viceroy's House, built in New Delhi. The preservation of this superb place is a tribute to CADW.

TALGARTH
St Gwendoline

The Church of St Gwendoline stands at the highest end of Talgarth, a small market town that lies between the Brecon Beacons and Black Mountains.

The church comprises a 15th-century tower, and a main body that dates from around 1400. Originally built to a transeptual plan, the south transept was subsumed into a new south aisle at the end of the Middle Ages, effectively creating a double-naved church. The north transept remains – used as a National School until the end of the 19th century, and now as a meeting room. Reuse of some 13th-century windows point to St Gwendoline's origins, and there is some speculation that the site may have been a Celtic 'clas'. The interior has been subject to an extensive Victorian reordering, with a wagon roof, tiled flooring and masonry work. In the south nave or aisle, on the southern wall of the chancel, there are two memorials: one to Joseph and Thomas Harris; the other to Howell Harris.

Howell Harris was a teacher who, during a communion service in 1735 at St Gwendoline's, experienced a revelation that converted him to Methodism. He became a fiery and dogmatic itinerant preacher, travelling throughout central and southern Wales, sometimes in the face of daunting public hostility. Harris was heavily criticized for his dogmatic obstinacy, as well as for his relationship with the self-proclaimed prophetess Mrs Sidney Griffith, who would later fund his new industrial and agricultural community at Trefeca.

Though he preached Methodism, Howell Harris remained wed to the principles of unity between the Revivalists, Moravians and the Anglican Church. Acrimonious differences of opinion between Harris and Daniel Rowlands, a fellow Revivalist Methodist preacher who had been expelled from his curacy for preaching outside his designated parish, led Howell Harris to retire from evangelical preaching. Instead, he turned his attention, with the help of Mrs Griffith, to the founding of 'The Family', a religious community based at his Breconshire birthplace. Here he invented agricultural machinery, founded a publishing house, and ran a rigorous and tough regime for the community members, who represented over 60 different trades.

The Howell Harris memorial stone

NEAR the Altar lie the Remains of
HOWELL HARRIS *Esquire*,
Born at Trevecka January the 23^d 1713/14 O.S.
Here where his Body lies, He was convinced of Sin,
Had his Pardon Sealed,
And felt the Power of Christ's precious Blood,
At the Holy Communion.
Having Tasted Grace, He resolved to declare to others
What God had done for his Soul.
He was the first itinerant Preacher of Redemption
In this Period of Revival in *England* and *Wales*.
He Preached the Gospel
For the Space of thirty-nine Years,
Till He was taken to his final rest.
He received all who sought Salvation
Into his House.
Thence sprung up the Family at
Trevecka,
To whom He faithfully Ministered unto his end,
As an indefatigable Servant of GOD,
And faithful Member of the *Church* of *England*.
HIS END
Was more blessed than his Beginning.
Looking to Jesus crucified
He rejoiced to the last, that Death had lost its Sting.
He fell a Sleep in Jesus at *Trevecka* July 21st. 1773,
And now rests blessedly from all his labours.

UNDER the same *Stone* lie also the Remains of his late Wife
ANN HARRIS
Daughter of *John Williams*, of *Skreen Esquire*;
Who departed this Life March 9th 1770, *AGED* 58.
She loved the Lord Jesus, Relied on his redeeming
Grace and Blood, and with her last Breath declared her
Confidence in HIM.
They left one beloved Child, who was the constant
Object of their Prayers and Care, and who Honours their
Venerable Memory.

A'r doethion a ddisgleiriant fel disgleirdeb y ffurfafen; a'r rhai a
droant lawer i gyfiawnder, a *fyddant* fel y Ser byth yn dragywydd.
Dan. Pen. XII. Adn. 3.

GAMES fecit.

There was hard manual work and three daily services, the first of which was at 4 am each morning. Experimentation with agricultural techniques led him to be one of the initiators of the Brecknock Agricultural Society.

After Howell Harris's death in 1773, some 20,000 people attended the funeral, held at St Gwendoline's Church, where he was buried in front of the altar rails. Ironically, having unwittingly contributed to the separation of Methodism from the Anglican Church, he died a communicant of the Anglican Church in Wales. Trefeca, the home of his community, is now a museum and conference centre.

Nearby: Llanelieu, St Ellyw

TAL-Y-LLYN
St Mary FoFC

This lonely little church on the Isle of Anglesey has recently been rescued from redundancy. It is the chapel of ease to the nearby church of St Peulan; it is a simple building of medieval origin, and its modest size is accentuated by the extensive churchyard in which it sits. The communion

rails and pulpit are 18th century, and
the open-back paddle-ended pews are
re-carved contemporary versions of
the originals, which were stolen
during the time that the church was
redundant.

St Mary's chapel of ease is worth
visiting, not so much for its architecture and history, rather for its simplicity and lonely setting.

Nearby: Llanbeulan, St Peulan

WREXHAM
St Giles

The Church of St Giles in Wrexham is
a significant medieval church, and the
largest such in Wales. Oddly, it seems
to be better known in the United Sates
than in Britain, largely due to the burial in the churchyard of Elihu Yale. Yale
came to England from the American
colonies at the age of four, later he
became a highly successful merchant,
and was eventually appointed
Governor of Madras, a position from
which he was relieved as a consequence of his questionable business
ethics. Yale became the principle benefactor of the university that would
bear his name and Wrexham Tower at
Yale University is a replica of the
tower of St Giles's, Wrexham.

St Giles's, the third church on the
same site, was built in the 1500s in
the Perpendicular style. Its imposing
tower, some 135 feet high and visible
for many miles around, is known as
one of Wales's 'Seven Wonders'.

Inside the church, a long nave is
flanked by two aisles, both lit by well-
proportioned and airy Perpendicular
windows. On the wall of the north
aisle is a melodramatic memorial to
Mary Middleton, by the Anglo-French
Rococo sculptor Louis-Francois
Roubiliac, whose other works include
a statue of Handel for London's
Vauxhall Gardens, and Westminster
Abbey's Nightingale monument,
arguably one of the most hideous
pieces of monumental sculpture in
existence.

Unusually for a church in the
Perpendicular style, the chancel is
apsidal in shape, like the Church of
St Mary in nearby Mold. Above the
chancel arch can be seen traces of a
16th-century painting of the Last
Judgement, and from a nearby roof
boss a painted devil's head peers
down. The roof space bears close
scrutiny, being decorated with a small

host of beautifully carved Tudor musical angels, brightly painted and seeming almost to be in perpetual flight. An equally colourful, but more contemporary roof feature painted by local schoolchildren can be seen in the roof boss under the tower.

St Giles's Church is a true survivor: having managed to transcend Cromwell's barbaric and demeaning custom of stabling horses therein, it was also rescued from the misguided reordering intentions of Victorian clergymen by the intervention of William Morris. Although Wrexham is a ghastly town into which to venture by car, an opportunity to visit this splendid church should not be passed up.

Scotland

More than anywhere else in the British Isles, Scotland's churches tell a story of historical, religious and political change. Conflict with the English, Calvinism, the suppression of Catholicism, the English oppression of the Covenanters and the Jacobite uprisings all contributed to disruption and destruction. For this reason some disused and some ruined churches are included, though to a lesser extent than in the Ireland section.

Two principal Scottish organisations are concerned with the restoration and conservation of churches of architectural and historical interest – the Scottish Redundant Churches Trust and Historic Scotland. I feature churches from both organisations. These include Auchterarder's Tullibardine Chapel – deep in the remote Perthshire countryside, but a church in a near perfect state with a melancholy lack of purpose – and Cromarty East Church, which is in the process of restoration and looking as if the congregation has only recently walked out. In vivid contrast, and in no one's care, is the site of the Chapel of St Columba at Kilneuair, high above the banks of Loch Awe. This is the hardest church site to get to; it is also the most ruinous and certainly the most mysterious.

One particularly striking early 20th-century church stands out – St Laurence in Forres. It is a wonderful mixture of exuberance and moderation in a land whose traditions of church building have in recent centuries been characterised by liturgical and architectural restraint. There are some glorious restorations too, exemplified by the collegiate Church of St Mary in Haddington, which, incidentally, also wins my award for Scotland's most welcoming church.

The variety of churches in the Scottish religious landscape is fascinating, all the more so because everything is so bound up in the history of the country, a compelling synthesis of landscape setting, architectural interest, historical significance, and, in the case of The Italian Chapel at Lambholm on Orkney, a moving tale of faith and improvisation.

List of Churches

Auchterarder, Tullibardine Chapel
Aberdour, St Fillan
Benholm, Old Kirk
Bonkyl, Bonkyl Kirk
Cromarty, Cromarty East Church
Culross, Culross Abbey
Dallas, St Michael
Dunglass, The Collegiate Church of
   St Mary the Virgin
Dunning, St Serf
Edinburgh, The Kirk of the Greyfriars
Edrom, Church of the Virgin Mary
Fordyce, St Talarican
Forres, St Laurence
Golspie, St Andrew
Haddington, St Mary
Inchcolm Island, Inchcolm Abbey
Isle of Bute, St Blane
Isle of Whithorn, St Ninian
Keillmore, Keills Chapel

Kilmartin, Kilmartin Parish Church &
   the Portalloch Stones
Kilneuair, The Chapel of St Columba
Kinneff, Kinneff Old Kirk
Kirkton, The Craignish stones and chapel
Kirkwall, St Magnus
Lambholm (Orkney), The Italian Chapel
Largs, St John
Loch Awe, St Conan
Macduff, Macduff Parish Church
Marnoch, Marnoch Old Kirk
Monymusk, St Mary
Pluscarden, Pluscarden Abbey
Preshome, St Gregory
Roslin, Rosslyn Chapel
Rothesay (Isle of Bute), St Mary
Tibbermore, Tibbermore Church
Torpichen, Torpichen Preceptory
Tranent, Tranent Parish Church
Tynet, St Ninian
Whithorn, Whithorn Priory

KIRKWALL

LAMBHOLM

GOSPIE

PLUSCARDEN

PRESHOME

CROMARTY

MACDUFF

FORDYCE

FORRES

TYNET

DALLAS

MARNOCH

MONYMUSK

KINNEFF

BENHOLM

LOCH AWE

TIBBERMORE

KILNEUAIR

AUCHTERARDER

KEILLMORE

KIRKTON

DUNNING

CULROSS

ABERDOUR

HADDINGTON

KILMARTIN

ROTHESAY

TRANENT

INCHCOLM

TORPHICHEN

EDINBURGH

DUNGLASS

LARGS

ROSLIN

BONKYL

ISLE
OF
BUTE

EDROM

WHITHORN

ISLE OF WHITHORN

AUCHTERARDER
Tullibardine Chapel HS

Hidden behind a screen of pine trees, under the broad skies of the Perthshire countryside, Tullibardine Chapel is one of very few complete medieval churches remaining in Scotland.

Sir David Murray of the Murrays of Tullibardine is believed to have built the church shortly before his death in 1450. It was built for family rather than parish use, suggesting a probable intention to create a collegiate church. The church was of a plain rectangular plan, typical of many rural churches in Scotland, with a choir, nave and west tower. It was left to a descendant, Sir Andrew Murray, to undertake the work that shaped the church as it is today: the nave was extended, a new tower built, and north and south transepts were added.

After the reformation, illegal masses continued to be held at Tullibardine Chapel but, in the 17th century, the Murray family moved away. They continued, however, to use the chapel as a place of burial.

Though only open in summer, Tullibardine chapel is now a place of quiet dignity, home to nesting swallows and empty of all furnishing but in good state of repair and in the most beautiful rural setting.

Nearby: Dunning, St Serf

ABERDOUR
St Filian

Sympathetically restored in the 1990s, this simple asymmetrical Norman church situated above Aberdour Harbour, with views to Inchcolm Abbey in the Firth of Forth, is one of the finest examples of plain Norman architecture in Scotland.

At least part of St Fillan's has been here since the early 12th century – the chancel and much of the north wall of the nave date from then. The church was enlarged by the addition of a south aisle in the 15th century. However, the Norman character of the church was preserved in this addition by the use of a series of bulky circular faux-Norman pillars in the arcade. Whether by chance or design, the stonework matches so well that one's first impression is that the south aisle

is an original Norman feature.

Everything here is plain: the stonework is coarse, but that adds to the charm of St Fillan's. The chancel has retained its deep-splayed Romanesque windows, and a 16th-century three-light window set in the west wall echoes the simplicity of the earlier windows.

In the 18th century the future of the church came under threat: a dispute over a choice of minister resulted in most of the congregation turning to the local Dissenting Meeting House. Then the Countess of Morton, of Aberdour Castle, decided that she didn't care for worshippers to be so close to the castle. St Fillan's church was closed, and a new parish church, more distant from the castle, was built. The roof of the church was removed and attempts were made to have the church levelled to the ground as it got in the way of the Countess's favourite pastime – hunting. This didn't happen, but the church remained a roofless ruin until 1926 when a major restoration took place; through a combination of gifts in kind and money, St Fillan's was re-roofed and refurnished. The original font was discovered in the churchyard, and was restored to the church. A church valued both for its architecture and its pleasing atmosphere was brought back to life.

BENHOLM
Benholm Kirk SRCT

Benholm Kirk was built in 1832. The appellation 'old' which is often applied to it might seem rather inappropriate since the original 13th-century church was dynamited to make way for it; in mitigation, however, there was a certain amount of salvage incorporated into the 'new' old church.

The kirk is a simple late Georgian structure, lit by generous arched windows. It sits in a mossy emerald-green churchyard, full of gently leaning tombstones shaded by trees. The interior is deliberately unembellished, in keeping with religious practice of the time. Priority was given to seating as many people as possible, and an extensive gallery allowed for 768 people to be accommodated, providing that they occupied no more than 16 inches of seating space each.

Items to be found here from the original church include a 15th-

century tabernacle, now set into the
east wall, and several monuments.
One of these, a low relief carved wall
monument, is dedicated to the Keith
family, and shows members of the family being pierced by Death's darts. One
figure is depicted holding his musket,
a sign of status in the early 17th
century when owning a firearm was
unusual. Another nearby monument
vividly shows how funerary sculpture
had developed by the later years of the
1700s: sweeping fabric folds, cherubs
and foliate detail in white marble
make an intriguing contrast with the
childlike depictions of the Keith
Monument.

BONKYL
Bonkyl Kirk

I came across Bonkyl Kirk quite by
chance, driving through the Scottish
Borders on an early summer day. It's
a plain rectangular Georgian church
with a bellcote above the west gable,
and lit by a range of arched windows
on the south side of the nave. Slightly
unexpected was the two-light faux-
Romanesque east window and, even
more unexpected, was the semi-
circular apse of a much older church
standing separately and to the south-

west of the church.

History is sketchy here, to say the
least. There was a church at Bonkyl in
the early 13th century, which fell into
ruins in the 15th century, although
services were still held there for a
short time. The old church, with the
exception of the apse, was finally
demolished in 1820, and the materials
were used to create the existing
church. This fine semi-circular apse,
however, suggests that the original

place for a local family.

The interior of the church is pleasant too: while it is mostly taken up with plain wooden pews and a gallery at the west end, the east end has been separated from the main body of the church by the construction of a neo-Romanesque chancel arch flanked on both sides by blind arcades. The two-light window at the east end balances very well with the chancel arch, creating an unusual feature in this type of church building. This is said to have come about during renovations work at the beginning of the 20th century under the minister of the time, the Revd Mair. In an interesting twist, it also brings into the Georgian church an echo of the apse in the churchyard.

Nearby: Edrom, Church of the Virgin Mary

church was much older than the 13th-century origins attributed to it, with a style more typical of the Anglo Saxon tradition. The fact that it was allowed to remain standing, when the rest of the church had been demolished is a mystery; it was latterly used as a burial

CROMARTY
Cromarty East Church SRCT

Seafaring is omnipresent in Cromarty. This ancient and historic town is perched at the tip of Cromarty Forth and history permeates its well-preserved streets and lanes. At the end of one such, Church Street, stands a plain T-shaped church – Cromarty East Church. It

was declared redundant in 1998, and is now in the hands of the Scottish Redundant Churches Trust, who are planning extensive repairs and restoration, although the everyday care is in the hands of local friends of the church.

First impressions are of a fairly

ordinary Scottish church, in a dilapidated state, set in a quiet and equally
dilapidated churchyard. It is not without charm, however, and is of historical significance, as the interior
provides a fine example of the nature
and impact of post-Reformation
changes in Scottish church practice.
After the Reformation, a complete
reordering of the interior emphasised
preaching, and the east end and altar
lost significance. All attention was to
be focused on the preacher, and to
this end a central pulpit with a large
sounding board behind was constructed midway along the south wall.
There is little if any decoration.

By the early 18th century, the
church was hardly able to accommodate the congregation, and an extension to the north was built, giving the
building its distinctive T-shape. This
extension contained a gallery, known
as the 'poor loft'. A few years later
another gallery was installed at the
east end – the 'Laird's Loft' – and the
'Scholar's Loft' above the west end
was rebuilt. At the same time seating
was installed under the galleries,
replacing an older custom whereby
the congregation brought stools
to church.

Frankly, the end result is rather
cheerless and cramped, but with
the rationale for the church being
to ensure that as many people as
possible heard the Word, Cromarty
East Church is an interesting historical
example of how many churches
functioned in Scotland after the
Reformation.

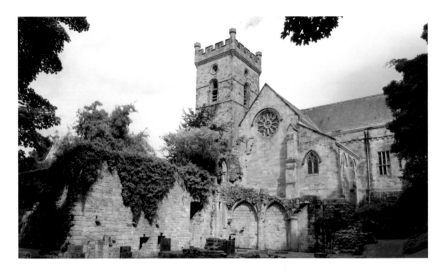

Culross Abbey HS

There are curious features about Culross Abbey. The Cistercians – the first known people to mine for coal on the nearby banks of the River Forth – founded the monastery in the 13th century. It is now part ruin, in the care of Historic Scotland, and part parish church for the town of Culross; it is also sited on a steep slope – an unusual choice of site that must have complicated the building process considerably.

There are two ways in. One leads into an open area of the ruins past the chapter house into the cloisters, of which some fine vaulting remains to the north. From here you have a 'worm's' eye view up the hill of the other remains of the monastery and of the present abbey church above, which can itself be puzzling as it is not of its original configuration. One needs to go up the hill and into the abbey church – the second way in – to try and make sense of this imbalanced appearance. The church that one sees today was the original choir and chancel of the abbey. West of the tower, the nave extended to a similar distance, and the adjoining Manse was constructed using recycled stone from the demolished western part of the Abbey.

DALLAS
St Michael

The present Church of St Michael in Dallas stands on the edge of the River Lossie in Moray, and dates from the end of the 18th century. It replaces an earlier heather-thatched church mentioned in records in 1226 and is believed to be the third church on the site. It was built in 1793, and the foundations of the church it replaced lie under the churchyard.

It is in the churchyard that the main interest lies: St Michael's Cross, the former medieval market cross, marks the site of a regular fair; and there is a curious stone building, much like a miniature cottage but actually a watch house. Its existence suggests a certain level of lawlessness or rowdy behaviour in the vicinity of the church: the watch house would have been used variously as a shelter for a night watchman, or as a lock-up for miscreants.

Nearby: Forres, St Laurence

DUNGLASS
Dunglass Collegiate Church HS

Just north of Cockburnspath is a fine, restored collegiate church ruin, dedicated to St Mary the Virgin.

The church was founded in the 15th century by Sir Alexander Home: its initial form was of a nave and chancel. The 16th century saw construction of a central tower and transepts, and, by the Reformation, the collegiate included a provost and twelve priests.

The church continued in use until the 18th century, when it was used as a barn. The remarkable state of preservation owes a lot to the sturdy stone-vaulted roof, and the building sometimes seems as though it is simply waiting for the windows to be glazed again in order to resume its former life.

Nearby: Haddington, St Mary

DUNNING
St Serf HS

The distinctive Romanesque tower of St Serf's Church, with its saddleback roof, stands above the little village of Dunning; it is a rare survivor of the Jacobite retreat from the battle of Sheriffmuir when most of the village was burnt to the ground.

Gilbert, Earl of Strathearn, built this

simple dignified church some time around the 1200s. The tower is its most distinctive external Norman feature, while the chancel arch is the principal remaining sign of Norman construction inside. The church underwent radical alterations in the late 17th century, with a gallery and external stairs being installed, and, in the early 18th century, substantial rebuilding work created the present T-shape. This shape draws one's attention towards a grand pulpit and deacons' chairs midway along the south wall of the old nave.

In the chancel can be seen the Dupplin Cross, brought in for conservation from the site of a nearby ancient Pictish royal palace. It is an outstanding piece of 9th-century carving, and is thought to be dedicated to Constantine, King of the Picts. Crosses of this type are plentiful in Ireland, but this is the only complete example from early Pictland. The detail of the cross is breathtaking. Apart from the scrolled vine motifs and knotted patterns, it shows King Constantine; an interesting convention of the time, and well illustrated here, is the deliberate exaggeration of the size of his head and moustache, which denotes elevated social status. Compare his figure with those of four warriors underneath: no moustaches, and heads more in proportion to their

bodies. Elsewhere on the cross shaft there is a dynamic depiction of hunting dogs, biblical scenes, and further

decorated motifs owing much to the Northumbrian style of carving. On the back of the cross shaft is a Latin inscription that translates as 'Constantine, Son of Fergus'. This is

a rare treasure, but do take time to look at the church too.

Nearby: Auchterarder, Tullibardine Chapel

The Kirk of the Greyfriars

This much-visited church in Edinburgh's Old Town is surprisingly plain for a building of such imposing size. It was named after a nearby pre-Reformation Franciscan friary, and the original building was the first post-Reformation church built in the city, and was completed in the early 17th century. Though it played a significant role in Scottish religious history, the rather morose rectangular kirk has an idiosyncratic history: the kirk one sees now was once two churches within the same building.

The original tower, used by the town council as a gunpowder magazine, blew up in 1718, demolishing the whole of the west end. The remaining east end was sealed off, and a new kirk was built out from the new west wall, creating two churches under the same roof. They were called respectively Old Greyfriars (the surviving eastern part), and New or Wester Greyfriars.

Some attempt at architectural detail was made at this time: a Palladian portico gave access to both churches, and the buttresses were topped with carved finials. However, the rebuilding didn't survive long: a fire in 1845 caused extensive damage. The new kirk was restored in short order, but the old kirk had to be rebuilt, during which it acquired a single span roof and Early English-style lancet windows. Not until 1932 were the two parts reunited, forming once again a single church.

Outside, the graveyard is full of interest. In 1638 the kirk had been the setting for the adoption of the National Covenant, a declaration that challenged the Stuart belief in the Divine Right of the Monarch to be the spiritual head of the Church of Scotland; the Covenanters affirmed their conviction that only Jesus Christ could ever be the spiritual head of a Christian Church. The Covenanters'

Prison, where over 1,000 Covenanters were incarcerated awaiting either execution or transportation for daring to sign the National Covenant, lies in the northeast corner of the churchyard.

There is a monument commemorating the covenanters as well as many other interesting monuments and memorials to such notables as the celebrated physician Archibald Pitcairn. Pitcairn was a prominent Jacobite who was buried with a quantity of wine that was to be disinterred and drunk only on the restoration of the Stuarts (it is said that the wine was drunk at the renovation of his tomb in 1800). One other fascinating feature of the kirkyard is the collection of memorials and tombs on the perimeter, which are erected against the backs of the adjoining artisans' houses, effectively blocking out daylight from their lower windows.

Nearby: Roslin, Rosslyn Chapel

EDROM
Church of the Virgin Mary

The present Edrom Parish Church, though mostly 19th century, has parts

that date from 1732. They in turn replace an older Norman church – the Church of the Virgin Mary – from which there are two remarkable surviving features: the first is the 15th-century Blackadder Aisle, incorporated into the church at the time of its rebuilding (regrettably viewable by prior arrangement only); the second is the Edrom Arch (left).

The arch is the Norman doorway to the original church, recycled as a burial vault and sited to the rear of the church. Deprived of the protection of a hood-moulding in its original setting means weathering has affected the arch's detail, but it still bears three orders of chevron and square carved patterns, which give a hint of the splendour of the original church. The arch is sunk below ground level, access being by steps down, and then steps up into the vault, allowing a good view of the arch from underneath.

Nearby: Bonkyl, Bonkyl Kirk

FORDYCE
St Talarican

Dedicated to a Pictish saint, the remnants of the Church of St Talarican are on an ancient site in the shadow of Fordyce Castle. The churchyard and church remains are captivating, and seldom visited.

Next to a 16th-century tower house in the town lies a small churchyard, containing the now disconnected remnants of the 15th-century church. Records of a church exist from 1272, but it is very likely that there has been a church here from much earlier. St Talarican's Church has been rebuilt several times since then, and, though there are now only fragmentary remains, they nevertheless possess considerable charm.

The churchyard contains many interesting tombstones and memorials, but is dominated by a small gable-ended building, topped by a stone belfry. This is both the ancient porch of the earlier church, and the session house (a place where church matters were discussed, also sometimes used as a schoolroom).

To the east of the belfry are remnants of the south side of the church, now divided into two, and containing memorials to two local families.

Nearby: Marnoch, Marnoch Old Kirk

St Laurence

The busy town of Forres was once home to a 12th-century chapel built by Alexander III of Scotland in memory of his wife, and dedicated to St Laurence, the patron saint of Forres. Most of the ideas for its modern successor came from the Revd. Alexander Buchanan, who left the Church of Scotland for a priesthood in the Scottish Episcopal Church.

St Laurence's Church is a recent church for such an ancient site. Built between 1904 and 1906, it is a neo-Gothic church of epic proportions, whose spire looms some 120 feet above the town. The quality of the stone masonry is outstanding, eschewing austerity for a restrained flamboyance exemplified outside by the pinnacles with carved finials that crown the length of the nave. Inside, the church is even more unusual: a broad south aisle with a large upper gallery flanks the nave. The gallery is an excellent spot from which to get an impression of the spaciousness of St Laurence's Church and to get a closer look at the craftsmanship of the carved pitch-pine hammerbeam ceiling. All the windows contain stained glass, and the windows in the south wall by Douglas Strachan, a painter turned stained-glass maker, are particularly good examples of modern stained glass in a traditional style. The themes represented include the Resurrection, Crucifixion and Ascension. Notice the pelican in the Crucifixion window – a symbol of sacrifice – and, towards the bottom of the Resurrection window, is a phoenix, the symbol of immortality and rebirth.

One might be forgiven for thinking that the church was Byzantine in nature rather than Church of Scotland, especially when coming across the baptistry pierced into the chancel archway on the south side, where marble steps lead up to a simple space containing a white marble font modelled on its counterpart at Dryburgh Abbey. The octagonal pulpit carved from Caen stone is also an exotic flourish in this pleasing building.

Nearby: Dallas, St Michael

GOLSPIE
St Andrew

Built in the 1730s as an estate church for the Earls of Sutherland, St Andrew's Church stands on the site of a number of earlier churches dating back to the 13th century. It is of interest in itself, but is particularly worth seeing for its setting against the impressive backdrop of the North Sea.

The present church is much as it was, with the exception of a south aisle, which was added in the mid-18th century. It is thought by many to be one of Scotland's best examples of a small post-Reformation church. The focus is on the preaching of the Word and the central pulpit canopy was carved by Kenneth Sutherland, the estate joiner. He also constructed a gallery for the Earls of Sutherland with a room behind into which they could retire between services.

The churchyard has an extensive range of tombs and memorials, some of considerable age, and many bearing macabre carved representations of Death ubiquitous in Scottish burial sites. St Andrew's is a fine place that combines an impressive landscape setting with the atmosphere of a simple style of worship in an early Georgian church.

HADDINGTON
St Mary

This extensive and venerable sandstone building, the largest of Scotland's parish churches, was only returned to active use in its entirety after one of Scotland's most significant 20th-century church restoration projects.

In the 16th century Henry VIII's English army left the transepts and choir of St Mary's in ruins, roofless

and at the mercy of the elements; the bold and highly successful restoration project of the 1970s reunited the nave and aisles, crossing, transepts and choir. The result is a parish church of cathedral-like proportions.

Externally it is difficult to tell that St Mary's is anything but a venerable church from the Middle Ages, although the stonework now includes stone from the demolished Caledonian Railway station in Edinburgh. Inside, too, old and new mix seamlessly with each other, although the stonework in the choir is clearly more weathered than that of the nave. Victorian furnishings coexist comfortably with medieval features, and the choir vaulting, made using fibreglass and marine technology, is a perfect companion for the vaulting in the nave.

Excellent glass abounds throughout. Handmade clear glass in the choir contrasts with some very good late 19th- and early 20th-century stained glass. A fine Burne-Jones window that started life in St Michael's Church, Torbay, was installed in the south transept, which also contains a pleasing contemporary stained glass by Sax Shaw. Another Burne-Jones window can be found in the south aisle. To the north of the choir is the misnamed Lauderdale Aisle (it is actually a chapel) containing an imposing marble family monument, as well as a set of simple painted wooden carvings depicting homage to the infant Christ by the three kings. There is a fine Orthodox icon from Mount Athos on the west wall.

St Mary's Church is a most welcoming place, alive with religious and cultural activity, and full of historical and architectural interest.

Nearby: Dunglass, Dunglass Collegiate Church

INCHCOLM ISLAND
Inchcolm Abbey HS

The ruined Augustinian abbey, in the care of Historic Scotland, is magnificently set on its own island in the Firth of Forth, and thus shares its setting with remnants of gun batteries and defences from the First and Second World Wars.

Several phases of development give Inchcolm Abbey its distinctive character: a simple two-cell church was constructed in the 12th century, and was later enlarged, separating the nave from the choir and chancel by a central tower. In the 13th century a north transept was added, and the choir was further extended, with a fine octagonal chapter house being built onto its south side. This early church was replaced in the 15th century. The nave was converted into monastic accommodation, and the new church was built eastwards, incorporating a large choir, new transepts and a presbytery. The cloisters, possibly the most complete in Scotland, were also built at this time and are unusual: rather than the more usual lean-to style of construction, they are fully enclosed – massive stone barrel-vaulted ranges pierced by deep window recesses.

Above the cloisters are the dormitory, refectory and warming room, and a later kitchen, while, to the southeast, is a group of buildings probably used as the abbot's residence. Elsewhere, particularly in the upper levels of the old church tower, large fireplaces and garderobes suggest accommodation for persons of importance.

This is a remote and wild site, home to aggressive nesting gulls and lethargic seals. It is only reachable by boat from nearby South Queensferry and is an excellent place in which to imagine the endeavours, hardships and trials of an isolated medieval monastic community.

ISLE OF BUTE
St Blane

St Blane's is a breathtaking monastic site situated on the southwest coast of the Isle of Bute. St Blane's Chapel is sheltered in a hollow surrounded by ancient oak and beech trees. A short but worthwhile uphill walk is required from the car park south of Kingarth to reach the site, from which there are fine views over the Sound of Bute to Kintyre and the Arran Hills.

An encircling drystone wall delineates the site of the monastery, at the centre of which stands a 12th-century Romanesque chapel. It was long thought to have been the original building on the site, but it is now known that the 12th-century facing stones of the chapel conceal the rubble stone remains of the basilica of St Blane, built in 575 AD. Excavations at the end of the 19th century uncovered a variety of artefacts – cross shafts and heads, burial slabs and, most memorably, a brass book clasp.

The chapel has retained some fine Norman features, despite centuries of exposure to coastal weather. There is a plain but well-proportioned two-order west doorway with intricate foliate carving on the capitals, and a finely decorated Norman chancel arch. The inner order of the arch is decorated with a beak-head motif, and the outer order bears chevrons enclosed by dog-tooth patterning. In the south wall can be seen a piscina set in a pointed arch recess, and set in the east wall is an aumbry.

Outside there are two burial areas. In the Middle Ages, the upper burial ground was used for monks, all men, while the lower was for lay people and women. Near the chapel is a much-weathered hog-back tomb-stone, thought at one time to be that of St Blane, but now known to be the 10th- or 11th-century burial stone of a Viking.

Nearby: Rothesay, St Mary

ISLE OF WHITEHORN
St Ninian

This roofless chapel, looking southeast over the sea towards distant Cumbria, was used as a place of reception for pilgrims landing on the coast en route for St Ninian's shrine.

The present building is 14th century, although studies have revealed the existence of an earlier 12th-century chapel, and it is known that, as early as the 6th century, pilgrims were making their way in-land to Whithorn to visit the shrine. It is the most evocative of sites – a place to picture the travel-worn sea-faring pilgrims gratefully coming ashore, safe in the knowledge that they were nearing their destination.

Nearby: Whithorn, Whithorn Priory

KEILLMORE
Keills Chapel HS

The Keills Cross

A small West Highland chapel, high above the shores of Loch Sween, houses one of the best collections of Celtic carvings in the West Highlands. Getting to the chapel requires some familiarity with single-track roads, but Keillmore brings ample rewards.

The chapel itself is of basic pattern, a single-cell building whose only discernible fittings are three aumbries in the east wall. The rounded arch of the window in the east wall suggests that the earliest part of the chapel may date from the late 12th century. Among the burial stones and stone carvings placed in here by Historic Scotland is the 9th-century Keills Cross, recently moved inside the chapel for protection against weathering. (A replica of the famous cross stands uphill from the chapel.) It is intricately ornamented on the shaft, with a large, circular 'bird's nest' boss at the centre of the enclosed cross. At the top of the shaft can just be made out the praying figure of a monk, while the side arms bear a motif of interlaced animals. Burial slabs placed around the chapel include examples from the 14th, 15th and 16th centuries.

KILMARTIN

Kilmartin Parish Church and the Poltalloch Stones HS

The parish church at Kilmartin is an
early Victorian church of limited
architectural interest, but, like the
nearby chapel at Craignish, it possesses one of the largest and oldest
collections of carved grave slabs in
Scotland.

The church is a replacement for an
earlier church and is situated in the
centre of Kilmartin Glen, an area
with a very high concentration of
prehistoric sites and ancient monuments. Many were carved by the
so-called Loch Awe sculptors, whose
work can also be seen at Craignish.
Though their work is widespread
through this part of the Western
Highlands, it is unlikely that the great
cross inside the church is attributable
to them.

The slabs date from between 1300
and 1700, and are in two main collections. The first group is under shelter
in a former burial aisle, while the
second grouping, known as the
Poltalloch Stones, is arranged in the
churchyard. The carving on these
stones is intricate and distinctive: on
some highly stylised foliate patterns
surmount animals, tools and imple-
ments, and enclose swords and
claymores; other slabs bear carved

The Poltalloch Stones

stone in front of the pulpit. At the Restoration some nine years later, they were disinterred and moved to Edinburgh Castle. They were not seen again until 1817, when Sir Walter Scott eventually discovered the 'Honours Three' in a locked chest in the Crown Room.

The Kirk was rebuilt again in the 18th century with three galleries. Space for the congregation was allotted according to property valuation, and an area in the centre of the church was reserved for communion and the rather menacing sounding 'place of repentance', where miscreants would be rebuked and admonished for their misdeeds.

KIRKTON
The Craignish stones and chapel

On a small hillock overlooking the broad expanse of Loch Craignish stands a small ruined chapel originally dedicated to St Maelrubha of Applecross. Inside is a collection of intricately carved stone slabs, known as the Craignish Sculptured Stones. A few miles southeast of Ardfern, it is easy to miss the small sign on the left-hand side of the road marking the site of the Stones; the chapel isn't indicated at all.

This modest little Norman chapel, roofless and overgrown, is almost unknown. It was abandoned in the 17th century, although burials continued to take place in the churchyard. Little remains: two deeply splayed plain Norman windows pierce the east-end wall, and there is a stone niche for use as a holy water stoup set by the south entrance. Two more niches can be seen in the east-end wall, which would probably have been used to house the chalice and paten used for mass. On either side of the chancel stand tomb chests dating from the first half of the 15th century. The end panels show a sculpted scene of the Crucifixion, and hunting scenes.

At the west end, under a lean-to shelter, is a small but excellent collection of sculptured stone slabs, preserved by the Natural History and Antiquarian Society of Mid-Argyll. There is a large base for a preaching cross, with a sundial; tomb slabs stand close by, bearing on them a sword, intricate interlocking motifs, and the depiction of a knight, also enclosed by a simple asymmetrical carved motif. They are the product of an active

school of stonemasons whose work is found up and down this picturesque coastline.

Nearby: Kilmartin, Kilmartin Parish Church and The Portalloch Stones

Carved stone slab depicting 14th century knight

KIRKWALL
St Magnus

St Magnus's Cathedral is a building of colour and levels: the contrasting red and yellow sandstone makes a rich pattern; and, inside, one's eye is constantly drawn up to the triforium and the lofty clerestory – an airy world of suspended levels.

The Cathedral of St Magnus is an extensive and richly detailed church: such a grand building in the remoteness of the Orkney Isles is surprising, but the Norse Earls of Orkney were powerfully influenced by contacts with European culture. There is a similarity here to Durham Cathedral, especially inside, and it is believed that masons from Durham may have been employed in the building of St

Magnus. Consequently the style here is predominantly Romanesque, with Early English refinements in the crossing arches and transepts. Inside the building is dark, largely due to the prevalence of typically small Romanesque windows, but this does not detract from the beauty of the interior, as the light takes on the characteristics of the richly coloured sandstone. The vistas within the cathedral are fascinating: though the building is small in comparison with other cathedrals, the masons' skill has created an impression of great height and everywhere there are views framed by complex and pleasing patterns of stone patterning, arches and columns.

The church is full of interest: against the inside walls stand many 17th-century tombstones, whose lettering and carving is in remarkably good order. The oldest tombstone, dating from the 13th century, is situated in the choir. In the south choir aisle is the ornate marble tomb of the Orcadian Arctic explorer John Rae.

Perhaps the best way to appreciate the artistry of the masons, and the uncanny sense of height and airiness in this deceptive space, is to explore the cathedral at its upper levels. Access is via some tight and confined spiral staircases, but it is worth the effort, giving truly magnificent views through a space that deceives the eye in its simple artistry.

Nearby: Lambholm, Orkney, The Italian Chapel

LAMBHOLM, ORKNEY
The Italian Chapel

This chapel is an extraordinary testimony to faith, and to the goodwill of the commandant of a prison camp for Italian POWs. In 1942, Italian troops captured in the North African campaign were sent to the Orkney Islands to help construct the 'Churchill Barriers', a series of barriers designed to protect the eastern approaches of Scapa Flow. Among the prisoners was an artist, Domenico Chiocchetti, who, together with several other prisoners, created a chapel for the camp. There was no question of using new materials, so the whole project was a miracle of improvisation, based on the use of scrap and salvage.

Two unlovely Nissen huts were joined, one for the sanctuary and the other for the 'nave'. Altar, altar rail and holy water stoup were moulded from concrete; candelabra were made from scrap metal; wood obtained from a shipwreck was used to make the tabernacle. Chiocchetti painted the vaulting of the sanctuary and the retable (the shelf behind the altar for ornaments), and Palumbi, another prisoner who had been an ironworker, constructed the wrought-iron rood screen – a work of outstanding craftsmanship. Chiocchetti and the other prisoners set to work in the nave, painting plasterboard to resemble brickwork.

They then turned their attention to the exterior: a facade of concrete was built, complete with a portico with an inset head of Christ; it was surmounted by a small belfry. At the same time the outside surfaces were coated in thick concrete.

Domenico Chiocchetti stayed behind at the end of the war to finish the chapel and, when he left, he was promised that the Orcadians would continue to care for it. Though they did, with the passing of time there was deterioration, and a preservation committee was formed. Domenico Chiocchetti was traced to his home village of Moena and in 1960, courtesy of the BBC, Chiocchetti returned to restore the painted interior – and deal with other urgently needed repairs. Before leaving, Chiocchetti

wrote a moving letter to the people of
Orkney, in which he said: 'The chapel
is yours – for you to love and preserve
… I shall remember always, and my

children will learn from me to love
you …'.

Nearby: Kirkwall, Orkney, St Magnus

LARGS
St John

Largs is best known as a dormitory
town for Glasgow, and as a coastal
tourist destination, but tucked away
on a corner overlooking a small green
and seafront promenade is an elegantly
proportioned church in an architectural style that has more in common
with France and Italy than Scotland.

St John's Church was established in
1843 and was a typical plain and utili-
tarian Free Church building – rectangular, with a small belfry. Towards the
end of the 19th century the young
architect Archibald J Grahame was
commissioned to design a new
church. He produced a design that
was both bold and elegant: a
Romanesque church in the Byzantine
tradition that incorporated three of
the original church walls. At the east
end an apse was constructed, and on
the northeastern corner of the church
an elegant campanile abutted a small
cloistral-style entrance with part-blind
Romanesque arcading. Douglas
Strachan, one of Scotland's finest

stained-glass designers, was commissioned to design three of the vestibule
windows.

Archibald Graham never lived to see
the fruits of his design, but St John's
Church stands as a fitting memorial to
a lost talent – its Byzantine elegance in
wry contrast to the surrounding bed
and breakfast establishments.

LOCH AWE
St Conan

Local tradition has it that St Conan's Kirk was built by Walter Campbell in the late 1880s so that his mother would not have a long drive to the nearest church.

The original church was modest, occupying what is now the nave. Campbell was not satisfied, however, and set out on what became a lifelong project to create a church of beauty, drawing on any architectural or decorative tradition that appealed to him. The work continued after his death in 1914, first under his sister, and then

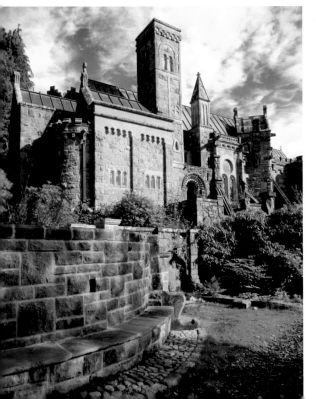

through a Trust.

Approached from the north, St Conan's Kirk gives the impression of being a relatively simple, if somewhat unusual, building. It is not until one walks round to the loch side that its eccentricity, fantasy architecture and decoration burst forth in an explosion of turrets, flying buttresses and stone ornamentation: Romanesque jostles with Saxon and Italianate; lead hares struggle to free themselves from the walls. The stonework is monolithic, comprising boulders found on nearby hillsides, and the whole church occupies a series of terraces that drop down to the waters of Loch Awe.

The kirk is entered through a cloister garth, and immediately one is confronted by the same eclectic approach that is evident outside. An apsidal chancel with Romanesque arches glitters with light from clear windows, through which distant mountains can be seen. Celtic, Early English, decorated and early Norman features predominate, and it might seem that St Conan's Kirk is an ecclesiastical and architectural nightmare. For me, however, it is a building of unexpected beauty, an expression of individual artistry and inspiration.

Macduff Parish Church

Macduff is a windswept bustling fishing port on the northern Aberdeenshire coast. It is crowded with grey granite houses and over-looked by a hill on which stands a war memorial and Macduff Parish Church (also known as Doune church after an earlier name for the port), whose tower is ornamented with a decidedly eccentric clock.

The original church was constructed in 1805 under the patronage of the Earl of Fife, and, in 1865, the building was enlarged. The enlargement work included a square section Italianate tower crowned with a cupola; the town clock was installed in the tower, but, rather than becoming the prop-erty of the church, it remained (and still remains) in the ownership of the burgh. Some views of the tower show that the architect had allowed for a clock with four faces but practical considerations, perhaps determined by the town purse, mean there are only two faces. One looks east towards the town, the other looks north, out to sea so, while Macduff Church tells the time for the townspeople and those at sea, those who live to the south or west have to rely on their own timepieces.

appearance, construct a new church.

On the outside this is a restrained 18th-century building, with the exception of an apsidal sanctuary, and a more ornate Baroque west entrance with pedimented gable (discreetly screened by surrounding trees). The interior belies the modest exterior, with an atmosphere redolent of both the Baroque and the Byzantine. The sanctuary was designed by Peter Pugin, son of the renowned Victorian champion of Gothic church restorations.

St Gregory's Chapel bears interesting testimony to the revival of Scottish Catholicism, as well as being a building of considerable elegance and beauty.

Nearby: Tynet, St Ninian

ROSLIN
Rosslyn Chapel

Rosslyn Chapel is surrounded by an aura of mystery, some of it inspired by speculative historical fiction, and some by its historic associations with Freemasonry and the Knights Templar.

Rosslyn Chapel's founder Sir William

St Clair originally intended to build a collegiate church of cruciform plan. But, following his death in 1484, the original plans were never completed.

What remains is extraordinary enough: the richness of the stone carving inside the chapel is breathtaking. From the Apprentice Pillar with its fluting overlaid by ornate spiral carving of the highest quality, to the riot of ornamentation on the vaulted roof of the Lady Chapel, with the recurrent Green Man theme (over one hundred in total throughout the building), the ornamentation demands one's closest attention. The more restrained north aisle contains the tomb of Sir William St Clair and the monument to George, Earl of Caithness. Here too are carvings of dragons, angels and demons, as well as depictions of scenes from the Gospels.

The barrel-vaulted choir roof is a work of epic ornamentation. Divided into five compartments, each separated by a transverse carved rib, the carving in four sections is based on different flowers, while the fifth – at the west end of the choir – is a star motif.

Extraordinarily, the chapel survived the Reformation, use as a stable by Cromwell's troops, and incursions by locals intent on destroying 'Popish' items during the reign of William and Mary, and it remains a remarkable

example of intricate stone carving and a testament to the skills of bygone masons and the vision of their masters.

Nearby: Edinburgh, The Kirk of the Greyfriars

St Mary

St Mary's was built in the 14th century as the parish church for the northern half of the island of Bute. The chancel – all that remains of the original church – is annexed to the 18th-century United Church of Bute.

An unusual carved baptism scene in the churchyard

Inside, and of particular interest, are the Knight's Tomb and the Lady's Tomb, set respectively in the north and south walls. Of the two the Lady's Tomb is the older, dating from the early part of the 13th century.

The adjacent United Church building is of no particular merit, but the graveyard is well worth exploring. There is a red sandstone mausoleum of awkward monolithic proportions to the north, while, near the entrance to the old chancel, casually propped against a wall, an intricately carved baptismal scene of unknown origin gently and regrettably moulders in the elements.

Nearby: Isle of Bute, St Blane

Tibbermore Church SRCT

Tibbermore church, set in beautiful rolling Perthshire farmland, is rather more than its dour post-Reformation appearance would at first glance suggest.

The present church dates from 1632, having been rebuilt on the site

of an earlier medieval church. Outside are many interesting memorials, one of which – to a James Ritchie – depicts his prize bull and curling paraphernalia. Surmounting the west gable is an unusual belfry, in the form

of a stone cage. A north aisle, erected
for workers from a nearby textile
printing company, was added in 1810,
giving a T-shape to the church.

Inside, 18th-century galleries face a
central pulpit, and in the late 19th
century a horseshoe style of seating
was introduced. All in all, some 600
worshippers could be accommodated.
Thought to be unique to such a modest rural church, stained-glass memorial windows commemorate the role
of women in the First World War.

This forlorn country parish church
is now thankfully in the hands of the
Scottish Redundant Churches Trust,
and an appeal is under way to raise
restoration funds.

TORPICHEN
Torpichen Preceptory HS

This doughty building, now in the
care of Historic Scotland, was the
Scottish headquarters of the Knights
Hospi-taller of the Order of St John of
Jerusalem from the 13th century until
the suppression in 1554. It was one
of only two major Hospitaller sites
in Britain.

The order was born when they
founded a hospital to cater for poor
and sick pilgrims to the Holy Land.
Recognised by Pope Paschal II in 1113,
the order acquired a distinct military
aspect when called upon to defend
pilgrims against attack, for which the
rewards were grants of land throughout Europe. A priory was founded in
London, and the order was granted
Torpichen by King David I of
Scotland.

The Preceptory nave, tower and
transepts, date from the late 12th
century, although the transepts and
nave were rebuilt in the 15th century.

Of the extensive range of domestic buildings, only the foundations now remain, and the survival of the transepts and towers may owe a lot to their being used as a courthouse after the Reformation. At the same time the nave was incorporated into the parish church. In the mid-18th century it was demolished to make way for a Presbyterian kirk of plain style, itself a pleasing example of the architecture of the time, complete with an external private staircase for the Laird's loft.

Although one may bemoan the loss of the nave and domestic buildings of a building of such antiquity, it is interesting to find a site where ruin and active parish church are physically and historically intertwined.

TRANENT
Tranent Parish Church

On a site dating back to 1145, the churchyard of this mining community's parish church contains a wealth of fascinating tombstones, monuments and grave slabs.

The church itself – which has its origins in the 15th century – is not without interest, with a trace of medieval walling in the lower courses of the walls, and a 16th-century window in the ruined burial aisle that projects from the north wall.

Presbyterian sobriety is interrupted by
a battlemented west tower, evidence
of an imaginative mason in a time of
austere church architecture.

Back in the churchyard, tombstones
bearing macabre skeletal figures jostle
with stones bearing symbols of the
trades of those they commemorate:
fletcher, divider and measuring stick.
An imposing memorial to members
of the Vallance family stands near the
entrance to the churchyard, an open
table tomb ornately carved with
cherubs is on the south wall of the
church, and there is a delightful headstone with a dormant scholar, and
another with impish ruff-collared
faces. This is a churchyard to explore
at leisure.

TYNET
St Ninian

This is an extended sheepcote, a
church in disguise in order to allow
covert worship. It is also the oldest of
the post-Reformation Scottish
Catholic churches still in use today.

In the strongly Catholic area of
Banffshire, there stood a long barn,
whose harled walls, plain windows
and thatched roof hid a secret church.
It was adopted as a place of worship
after the nearby church was burnt to

with its incomparable Hiberno-Romanesque west doorway, to the extraordinary Church of St Malachy in Belfast, uninspiring and frankly ugly on the outside, but with an outstanding and highly unusual interior. From ruin to active church, Ireland's churches impart a sense of mystery and continuity, rich in history, legend and architecture.

List of Churches

Adare, St Nicholas
Adare, Trinitarian Abbey
Ahenny, High Crosses
Ardmore, St Declan
Belfast, St Malachy
Clonfert, St Brendan
Clonmacnoise, Co. Offaly
Croom, Monasteranegh Abbey
Crossgar, Saul Church
Downpatrick, Down Cathedral
Downpatrick, Inch Abbey
Ferns, Ferns Cathedral
Freshford, Ballylarkin Abbey
Glendalough, St Kevin

Gowran, St Mary
Graiguenamanagh, Duiske Abbey
Kells (Co. Kilkenny), Kells Priory
Kells (Co. Meath), St Columba
Kells (Co. Meath), St Colum
    Cille's House
Kilkenny, St Canice
Kilree, Round Tower
Loughinisland, Loughinisland Churches
Thomastown, Jerpoint Abbey
Thurles, Holy Cross Abbey
Tullaherin, Kilfane Church
Waterford, Christ Church

ADARE

St Nicholas

The 'Black Abbey' of Adare, named after the black habits of the Augustinian canons, was founded by the Earl of Kildare in 1315. The friars left the abbey at the dissolution in the 16th century, after which time the buildings deteriorated considerably. The Dunraven family restored the abbey in the early 19th century, passing it over to the Church of Ireland for parish use. The prevalent style, notwithstanding the restoration, is Early English.

A topographical dictionary of the mid-19th century described the abbey ruins as 'Very extensive and highly interesting: they consist of the nave, choir, and south transept of the church, which, with the exception of the roof, are tolerably entire … the cloisters are nearly in a perfect state …'.

Much has changed since the 19th-century restoration, but the abbey retains a sense of dignity and luminosity. The cloisters are almost entirely unchanged, as if no one quite knew what to do with them. They enclose an overgrown garth; a struggling yew stands in the centre. Leading off the cloisters are damp and mossy passages, from which steep and irregular stone steps lead to locked doors. Here too, is the Quin family mausoleum. Various offices and outbuildings now house a school. The old entrance from the cloisters into the church is blocked off, giving the impression that, while other parts of the abbey have acquired new life, the cloisters have stubbornly closed themselves to change.

Nearby: Adare, Trinitarian Abbey; Croom, Monasteranenagh Abbey

ADARE
Trinitarian Abbey

There are three abbeys in Adare: the old Franciscan friary; the former Augustinian friary, now the Church of St Nicholas; and the old Trinitarian Abbey, which serves the Catholic parish of Adare. This abbey was founded in the 13th century, and, due to the colour of the order's habits, was known as the White Monastery. In addition to its religious purpose, the order was also involved in the ransom and rescue of captive Christian crusaders.

The 15th-century central tower, one of the largest in southern Ireland, is short and thickset, and was a later addition to the 13th-century abbey. The present-day church comprises a spacious nave and chancel, and north and south transept, though, strictly speaking, the church is not cruciform: the tower spans both the nave and south transept. At the intersection of the stone-ribbed vaulting of the tower are several mischievous carved faces, and

the stonework here seems to be the earliest. This area is where it is easiest to capture the sense of the church prior to its 19th- and 20th-century restorations, both of which seem to have been a little heavy-handed: the cloister was substantially lost as the church was extended to the north, although the columbarium remains. In vivid contrast to its neighbour St Nicholas's, Adare's Trinitarian Abbey is regrettably cluttered, and retains little of its original monastic simplicity.

Nearby: Adare, St Nicholas; Croom, Monasteranenagh Abbey

AHENNY
High Crosses

Celtic High Crosses are striking and monolithic features of the religious landscape of Ireland, especially those at the site of the ancient monastery of

Kilclispeen, at Ahenny. These two crosses – the North Cross and the South Cross – are among the earliest of the Celtic High Crosses.

The common elements of most stone crosses are proximity to a monastic site, size, and the stone ring enclosing the cross. The Ahenny High Crosses are fine examples of Celtic stone carving: intricate braiding, cording and geometrical designs. The North Cross still bears its stone cap, and on the south face of the pediment there is a carving of Goliath being taken to Jerusalem by David. The South Cross has lost its stone cap, although the stone ring enclosing the cross is intact. Considering that both crosses are carved from sandstone, the surviving detail is remarkable.

The South Cross, Ahenny

ARDMORE
St Declan

This is one of Ireland's most romantic and spectacular religious sites – the buildings of St Declan's stand on the top of the 'Great Hill' overlooking the broad sweep of Ardmore Bay.

There are three buildings on this airy site: the oratory, which dates from about the 8th century; the church (also known as the cathedral), dating from the 12th century; and the round tower, also from the 12th century. St Declan's Oratory is to the seaward side of the church, down a small slope. It is a plain early stone building,

restored in the early 17th century. The Lugudeccas ogham stone, bearing the inscription 'LUGUDECCAS MAQI ... COI NETA SEGAMONAS' (Lugaid, son or grandson of Nia-Segmon), was found in the oratory gables and is now in the main church. Devotees of the cult of St Declan believe that a hollow in the southeast corner of the oratory marks the burial place of the saint.

The church is possibly the most interesting of the three buildings. On the exterior of the west wall, beneath a simple lancet window, there are a

series of intriguing Romanesque carvings. The upper row – a series of smaller sculptures set in a Romanesque blind arcade – is heavily weathered, but the figure of the Archangel Michael weighing souls can be discerned. The lower row contains carvings of Adam and Eve, the Adoration of the Magi and the Judgement of Solomon. These are set in a much broader arcade. Inside are the ogham stone found in the oratory, and a second ogham stone dedicated to AMADU, the loved one. This second stone has the longest ogham inscription known in Ireland.

The round tower stands 90 feet high, commanding a comprehensive view of the coast to the south, as well as over the surrounding countryside. In common with all other round towers, its entrance is elevated, and would have been accessed by a ladder that was drawn up into the tower in times of danger. It is one of the most complete and best-preserved round towers in the country.

BELFAST
St Malachy

Sir John Betjeman once described the Church of St Malachy, completed in 1844, as 'a many coloured cavern'. Situated in Belfast's old market

district, this is an extraordinary late Georgian/early Victorian, faux Gothic/Tudor church.

The original intention behind the building of St Malachy's was as the cathedral of Down and Connor. It was conceived on a grand scale, with the intention of accommodating some 7,000 people, but the funds for this great project were reallocated to try to alleviate the worst effects of the Great Famine that was sweeping through Ireland at the time.

The plans were modified, and the original sanctuary area of the intended cathedral church was adapted for use as a parish church, which helps to explain the unusual floor plan. Often inaccurately described as cruciform, the building is actually a large rectangular space, with the longest sides to the east and west. Two side altars flank the High Altar, and running in a sweep from north to south – the entire width of the church – is a gallery that effectively doubles the number of seats available for the congregation. The whole is lit by a series of pleasingly proportioned four-light Gothic windows.

Even though this is a truncated version of the original plan, the space is impressive, and overhead is the pièce de résistance: the ceiling has a marvellous pastiche of the ceiling of Westminster Abbey's Henry VIII chapel. The plasterwork, in dusty pink and white, is exquisite.

The outside is more challenging: mock Gothic battlements top rather dingy, reddish-pink brickwork, and, from a distance, one is not sure whether one is looking at a church or a Victorian waterworks.

CLONFERT
St Brendan

A first impression of St Brendan's Cathedral has one wondering what such a richly ornamented church is doing in the tiny village of Clonfert, a backwater in the peaty Shannon hinterland.

This 12th-century cathedral, now the parish church of Clonfert, occupies the former monastic site founded by St Brendan in the 6th century. It was a popular centre for scholars and, at its height, there were over 3,000 monks. As late as the 16th century, there was a flourishing college here; it was so popular that it was considered as a rival candidate to Dublin as the site for a national university.

*The Hiberno-Romanesque west doorway
at Clonfert*

The church itself was originally a basic cruciform structure. Of the two transepts, only the south remains, roofless and separated from the main body of the church. The chancel was a later addition.

The west doorway is the great treasure of St Brendan's. It is an outstanding example of Hiberno-Romanesque carving. Comprising seven orders – six with carved patterning, and a plain seventh inserted in the 16th century – the doorway is surmounted by a tall triangular pediment that serves as a dripstone. The bottom section of this is a blind Romanesque arcade containing carved heads, below a pleasing tiered carving containing more faces arranged in a triangular motif. The crooked splay of the original door-

jambs contrasts with the uprights of the 16th-century order. Along the capitals of the doorjambs run intriguing Scandinavian-looking animal motifs.

In the south chancel archway a carved mermaid blithely combs her hair, a symbol of the Saint's maritime voyages. The vestry is most unusual: a plain vaulted space with the imprint of the original wattle ceiling. There are a number of interesting tomb slabs in the nave, and a striking stone set in the south wall by the narthex, which bears carved Celtic lettering. The 13th-century east window is of great beauty.

St Brendan's Cathedral has a harmonious atmosphere – a sense of ease with the landscape and nearby village – that makes it an essential place to visit.

Nearby: Co. Offaly, Clonmacnoise

CO. OFFALY
Clonmacnoise OPW

This great Celtic monastic settlement stands more or less in the centre of Ireland, in an ancient glacial landscape of gravel ridges and raised peat bogs, and on the banks of the River Shannon. The remaining range of buildings is an extraordinary testament to survival

in the face of persistent violence and disruption over the centuries.

St Ciaran founded the original monastery in the mid-5th century, and, despite his death shortly thereafter, Clonmacnoise rapidly became an ecclesiastical centre of great significance. Its position was strategic: the River Shannon runs north–south, and it lies on the main east–west route through Ireland. Inevitably, Clonmacnoise attracted a large lay population, living in an extensive sprawl of wattle and daub buildings, of which nothing now remains. Of the monastic buildings, however, much of interest is left.

Despite Viking attacks and raids by the Irish, the period leading up to the 12th century was a productive time for the monastery. Sculptured crosses and stone slabs were produced, as were illuminated manuscripts and chronicles. It was around the 12th century that most of the stone churches and the round towers were also built. But, from then on, Clonmacnoise went into dramatic decline.

Though Clonmacnoise did escape the initial ravages of the Reformation, in 1552 the English garrison from Athlone devastated the entire settlement and, in the 17th century, Cromwell's army finished the process. Clonmacnoise fell into ruins.

The eleven churches at Clonmacnoise were typical of pre-Cistercian and Augustinian settlements, each church being associated with a different family or religious function. The 10th-century cathedral is of great interest, with a fine Perpendicular 15th-century north door, and on the outside walls one can see the putlog holes that held the timbers on which the floor of the original wooden scaffolding sat.

Typical of the Irish, rather than the Norman, tradition is Temple Melaghlin, with its deep-splayed Transitional windows surrounded by continuous stone mouldings. Temple Finghin is a Romanesque church with an integral and remarkably well-preserved round tower. Fine Romanesque decoration can also be seen on the doorway and chancel arch of the nearby Nun's Church: one of the voussoirs here bears a Sheila Na Gig. Temple Connor is the only church in use, and has been since the mid-1800s.

Temple Finghin from the cathedral

The High Crosses that are spread throughout the site are replicas; the originals have been moved under shelter elsewhere on the site, or taken to the National Museum of Dublin. The most notable of these is the Scripture Cross, with carved scenes in vertical panels.

Nearby: Clonfert, St Brendan

CROOM
Monasteranenagh Abbey

This enigmatic ruin, Manistir an Aonaigh, the monastery of the fair (and later Manister na Maighe, the monastery of the Maigue) stands a short distance from the village of Manister, like a crouching giant on the banks of the River Maigue.

This is a massive ruin, whose nave,

choir and chancel measure nearly 200 feet in length. The chancel arch survived long enough for the antiquarian John O'Donovan to comment in his notes for the Ordnance Survey, 'I had no idea that the Irish built such splendid arches before the arrival of the English.'

Monasteranenagh Abbey was at one time a monastery of some importance, whose estates were spread far and wide, and whose abbot sat as a spiritual peer in the English parliament. Tantalising blocks of masonry, stone fragments and ruined walls are spread far and wide, hinting at a substantial and extensive original site. However, the 16th-century defeat of the Geraldine rebel John of Desmond culminated in a brutal massacre of both monks and the local community and brought about an abrupt halt to life at Monasteranegh. Nothing more is known of life at the monastery after 1601.

One advisory comment: the site is unattended, and a local farmer has made attempts to block access from the nearby road.

Nearby: Adare, St Nicholas; Adare, Trinitarian Abbey

CROSSGAR
Saul Church

Saul Church, a modern interpretation of an early Irish church, stands in a soft rolling rural landscape on a hill overlooking Strangford Lough. On a sunny day the views are stunning, both of the church and from it.

The story has it that a local chieftain gave a barn on this site to St Patrick as his first Irish church. St Dumnis, one of St Patrick's disciples, subsequently founded a monastery here. The site is certainly very old: early gravestones with weathered engraved crosses dot the churchyard, and there is an enigmatic dry stone vault. A ruined stone wall adjacent to the church serves as a reminder that the Augustinians were here from the 12th century.

The present church is recent, built in 1933 to commemorate 1,500 years since St Patrick's arrival in Ireland. It is a simple two-cell nave and chancel church, designed in the Celtic tradition, with an integral round tower standing to the south of the chancel. An interesting Norman font stands in the northwest corner of the nave, bearing a simple, strong, upright carved motif. Within, the atmosphere is one of peace and calm, simple and uncluttered, in keeping with Henry Seaver's original 1930s design.

Nearby: Downpatrick, Down Cathedral; Downpatrick, Inch Abbey; Loughinisland, Loughinisland Churches

Down Cathedral

Also known as the Cathedral of The Holy and Undivided Trinity, this building stands prominent on Down hill, an unmistakeable landmark overlooking the city and surrounding countryside. This is, in the main, a relatively new building created from the destruction and rebuilding of this cathedral church, described in the 18th century by missionary John Wesley as an 'ancient and noble ruin'.

In the 12th century John de Courcy, the Norman conqueror of Ulster, replaced the Augustinian canons of Waterford with Benedictine monks from St Werburgh's in Chester. Little detail is known of this period, save for the fact that there was a church and round tower and that, by 1220, the church and monastery were in a poor state of repair; this was exacerbated by an earthquake some twenty years later.

At the beginning of the 14th century the cathedral was burnt by Edward Bruce, and more acts of destruction and reconstruction followed. Lord Grey, the Lord Deputy of Ireland, brought about the final destruction of the monastery and church, which he used as stables for his horses. For the next 200 years a succession of deans presided over a ruin.

Between 1789 and 1812 major rebuilding work was undertaken. One casualty of this was the nearby round tower, demolished to provide building material. But restoration work was not complete until the 1980s. Virtually nothing remains of the earlier church, except for traces of the 12th-century walls. The essence of the cathedral is that of the original 15th-century chancel, with its tower and narthex. Inside, the chancel (which effectively forms the main body of the cathedral) is divided into three aisles. The seating arrangements here are unusual. Under the pulpitum are the Chapter stalls; these face east towards the altar, and are known as 'returned stalls'. The choir stalls are modelled on the medieval tradition; and behind them are fine bow-fronted Georgian box pews. Facing each other are two thrones: one for the bishop; the other for the secular judiciary. This dates from the time when the Law Courts convened in the cathedral. The 11th-century granite font had been used as a watering trough until its rediscovery in 1927, and in the narthex there are several carved fragments of early stonework.

Down Cathedral's fame originally came from the alleged burial of St Patrick there. Outside, a modern carved stone slab marks the site where he is said to be buried.

Nearby: Crossgar, Saul Church; Downpatrick, Inch Abbey; Loughinisland, Loughinisland Churches

DOWNPATRICK
Inch Abbey

This tranquil, ruined Cistercian abbey is situated in the Quoile marshes in grassy meadowland. It was founded in 1177 by John de Courcy, a Norman turned Irishman, and champion of the cause of St Patrick.

The original monastery on this site was called Inis-Cumhscraigh, built in the 9th century. By the mid-12th century it had become defunct, depleted by both Viking and Irish raids. The new monastery acquired a distinctly English flavour: monks from Furness in Cumbria came over to help with the continuing construction works, and their presence swelled the community numbers to the extent that Irishmen were refused admittance. The monks were even accused of hunting down local Irishmen with spears!

The abbey is in the Early English style, and there is evidence of an early collapse of the transeptual tower (a not uncommon occurrence with the rule of thumb methods of construction employed at that time). After 1400 a stone screen cut off the transepts, and the original church was reduced to a single chapel.

The ruins that exist today are largely the result of excavations and repairs in the early 20th century, when cement was used to restore many of the architectural details. Particularly well preserved is the east end of the abbey. But not withstanding the lack of entirety, the abbey is a rewarding place to visit, in its marshland setting, from where a fine view of Down Cathedral on the distant hill can be enjoyed.

Nearby: Crossgar, Saul Church; Downpatrick, Down Cathedral; Loughinisland, Loughinisland Churches

Ferns Cathedral

Ferns was one of the focal points of religious activity in the ancient Kingdom of Leinster. The cathedral was built in the early 1200s, and its successor, St Edan's, is easily missed as one drives past on the busy N11 road that bisects the town.

Little remains of the original cathedral, which was destroyed by fire in the Elizabethan era; although the Queen ordered that it be rebuilt, only a part of the nave was completed. A further restoration – effectively a new building – took place in 1817. There are some modest indications of the older building, principally fragments of the nave walls of the 13th-century cathedral; in the north wall five of the original seven lancet windows can be seen, and one remains in the south wall.

More interesting are the churchyard, and the area to the east of St Edan's. The churchyard contains several plain High Crosses, and a small part of a narrow stone shaft, believed to mark the burial place of Dermot MacMurrough Kavanagh, 12th-century King of Leinster. The remains of what may have been the 13th-century monks' choir occupy the area to the east of the chancel of St Edan's, and it can be seen that this was once a build-

ing of considerable substance. At the western end of this space a carved Celtic stone slab is casually propped against a wall. The site has not been comprehensively investigated, so there is plenty of room for speculation.

Celtic stone slab at the western end of the ruined choir

FRESHFORD
Ballylarkin Abbey

For those whose expectations of an abbey church, even one in ruins, are of an imposing building, Ballylarkin Abbey will come as something of a shock. Blink as you are winding your way down the tiny lane that runs past it, and it will have gone. There is something almost organic about the remains of this modest and ancient church building: it stands gently crumbling at the edge of a field in the middle of nowhere, one of the many ruined churches in Ireland that are left to the processes of nature.

Adjacent to the ruins of Ballylarkin Castle, the abbey was built in the mid-12th century, probably by the Shorthall family. This roofless hulk contains some surprises. In the south-west corner there is an impressive triple sedilia, in fine state of repair, of late Transitional origin. Next to it is a later, more ornately carved piscina, and a rudimentary aumbry. The remains of a corbel table can just be made out along the top of the south and north walls. A pile of rubble outside the west wall is the only remaining indication that there was once a further building attached to the church. Ballylarkin Abbey is a place in which to sit quietly, to take an imaginary journey into this remote and lonely building's history.

Nearby: Thurles, Holy Cross Abbey

GLENDALOUGH
St Kevin OPW

This is a wonderful, lonely monastic site, lying at the confluence of the Pollanass and Glenealo rivers, in the heart of the Wicklow Mountains. Here there is a vivid sense of what an early monastic settlement would have been like, with a series of granite and slate buildings seeming to grow out of the landscape.

It is a well-visited spot, for good reason. There are two ways to view Glendalough: the first is by entering the site (and its excellent associated visitor centre); the second is by walk-ing in the nearby hills, which afford spectacular views of the monastery. Whichever you choose, go early or late in the day, and preferably not in high summer.

Founded by St Kevin, the settlement dates from the 6th century, and for over 500 years was a major seat of religious learning. The monastery eventually fell prey to Vikings who raided from their base in Dublin, but, in spite of extensive fire damage, the community continued until the early 13th century, at which time the

uniting of the diocese of Glendalough and Dublin diminished its importance. In 1398 the English finished what the Vikings had started; the monastery was left in ruins, although its use as a church and pilgrimage centre persisted.

The stone monastery buildings from the 10th and 12th centuries survive, and a large model in the visitor centre gives a good impression of the entire early settlement. The cathedral is the largest remaining building, with a late Norman chancel and sacristy. Remnants of decorative carvings can be seen on the chancel arch and east window. The priest's house, Romanesque in style, is a near-complete reconstruction, using the original stones.

There are five further churches within the site, the earliest being the church of Our Lady. It is a simple stone building, with a nave and later chancel. The east window retains its dripstone, and bears two carved heads, and the west doorway, a massive granite affair, has a saltire carved into the underside of the lintel. The Church of St Saviour (the most recent of the churches on the site) is a 17th-century restoration of the original 12th-century church. It has an interesting three-ordered Romanesque chancel arch, bearing finely carved capitals, and the east window has carved decorations including a lion, two birds with a human head held in their beaks, and a serpent.

Together with St Kevin's Church and its round tower belfry, St Kieran's Church, discovered in the 19th century, and Trinity Church, with its pleasantly proportioned chancel arch, the monastic site at Glendalough will amply reward an extended visit.

GOWRAN
St Mary OPW

Standing overlooking the little country town of Gowran, the Collegiate Church of St Mary is part ruin, part restored ex-parish church, and houses an outstanding collection of memorials, effigies and monuments.

The Church of the Assumption of the Blessed Virgin, to give it its proper name, is a fascinating mixture of architectural styles, dating from between the 13th and the 19th centuries. It was originally a collegiate church, and is distinguished by the impressive length of the now-derelict

nave and aisles, the generously proportioned chancel and a bulky crenellated square tower. The oldest parts of
the fabric are in the east wall of the
ruined nave, and the lower courses of
the massive tower. In the 19th century
the tower was incorporated into a
parish church, which was built to
replace the chancel. The Church of
Ireland ceased use of the parish
church in the 1970s.

The stonework in the nave is magnificent. In the south aisle are examples of some of the earliest-known
window tracery in Ireland, and
throughout this part of the church
there is fine stone carving, attributed
to masons under the direction of the
master mason known as the 'Gowran
Master'.

Inside the former chancel, there is
a series of grave slabs, tombs and
memorials dating from between the
5th and the 20th centuries. Of particular interest is the 1626 table tomb of
James Kealey and his wife Ellen Nash,
which bears on its top a shrouded
skeleton; carved panels depict scenes
from the Passion, and depictions of St
Patrick and St Peter. The earliest effigy
is dated 1253 and is of Radoulfus,
Rector of Gowran. It is thought to be
the earliest dated burial monument in
Ireland.

Among the other effigies and monuments are a pair of 16th-century table tombs bearing the damaged effigies of one and two knights respectively, and there is an appealing high relief carving of a female figure in a pleated gown, wearing a heart-shaped headdress. This is a highly interesting and very varied collection of funerary sculpture and carving, brought together in a building of considerable architectural merit.

Nearby: Kilkenny, St Canice; Tullaherin, Kilfane Church

GRAIGUENAMANAGH
Duiske Abbey

Duiske Abbey is an impressive example of Early English architecture: the nearest equivalent is Strata Florida Abbey in Wales. At its height it was one of the largest and most extensive of the Cistercian foundations in Ireland: the nave is over 200 feet long. It is now restored, but some of its most fascinating features lie literally underground.

In the 12th century the Earl of Pembroke invited Cistercian monks from Stanley in Wiltshire to found a monastery. The monastery reflected the typically industrious nature of the Cistercians: reclamation of moorland and bog allowed agriculture to be practised on a large scale, from which an extensive wool trade developed. The 16th century suppression brought monastic activity to a halt and eventually the monastery fell into disrepair

and ruin; its octagonal tower finally collapsed at the end of the 18th century, burying the greater part of the abbey floor to a depth of about five feet.

At the beginning of the 19th century, a clumsy, poorly funded and ill-considered restoration of the abbey was undertaken. The height of the walls was lowered in order to take a pitched roof, and a controversial decision was made not to go down to the original level of the floor. The results bore little resemblance to the original 13th-century abbey.

It was not until the 1970s that a more considered restoration adapted the existing fabric, sympathetic to the spirit of the original abbey church. The interior was reordered and the remaining arcades at the west end were reunited with the nave, although it was by this time impossible to recover the north and south aisles, which had originally run the full length of the church. A fine open-framed roof was constructed at the height of the original roofline, using medieval techniques of wedging and dowelling. Inside, fragments of the original tiled flooring can still be seen just inside the main entrance to the north, on the east side of the north transept and in the southeast corner of the choir. The springs of the original rib-vaulted roof at the crossing have been retained, as have the original sedilia.

In the south transept, a door leads down to a chamber that served as a baptistry. This is the original floor level, and contains a rare surprise – a superb Romanesque doorway, accidentally discovered in 1916, and used originally by the monks when they processed from the cloisters to the church. The door deserves closer examination, with fine foliate decoration on the Early English capitals, and good decorative carving on the inner orders.

Duiske Abbey is a fascinating story of a recent restoration under difficult circumstances that has succeeded in re-establishing a church of great beauty, in which the serenity of ancient monastic life is all around.

Nearby: Thomastown, Jerpoint Abbey

The subterranean Romanesque doorway and baptistry

KELLS, CO. KILKENNY
Kells Priory OPW

Seen from the south, Kells Priory seems to be an extensive fortified castle, rather than a former Augustinian priory. A formidable curtain wall, pierced at intervals with tower houses, hides all within from view.

There are two approaches to this majestic ruin: one from the south walking downhill to the curtain walls; and one from the north, walking from a watermill. This is the more pleasant, with the King's River flowing by, and a constant babble from the mill-race. A footbridge leads over the river and directly into the ruins. It is a place for those who like imagining, for, although the remains are substantial, the whole site was turned to farming after the dissolution and much of the area north of the priory and its precincts has been flattened. There is ongoing archaeology here, and some restoration works too.

There are two parts to the priory. The monastic precincts – the buildings closest to the river – originally stood on an island, with a stream to the south separating them from what is now known as Burgess Court. The priory is the oldest part, dating from the 12th century (and twice burnt down within the space of a hundred years). It was adapted and changed extensively during the following three hundred years, always, it would appear from the thickness of the walls and presence of arrow slits, with the expectation of trouble. Uphill, Burgess Court (known in the 15th century as Villa Prioris, the Priory Town) is defined by the enclosing curtain wall and tower houses, most likely accommodation for minor Irish nobility in the late Middle Ages. Its purpose seems to have been primarily defensive. There is also some interesting evidence to suggest that the roadway into the town of Kells passed here.

Nearby: Kilree, Round Tower

KELLS, CO. MEATH
St Columba

This is an odd church site, and full of contrast and interest: Celtic High Crosses stand in the churchyard of an 18th-century church substantially altered by the Victorians in 1856.

The site is very old, dating from the 9th century, when Columban monks from Iona came to Kells. Nothing remains of the monastery. The church was restored in the 16th century, and altered three more times. The result is a plain and uninspiring exterior, in complete contrast with the splendid Victorian reordering of the interior. The bell tower, the only surviving part of the 16th century church, is a curiosity. The spire, erected in 1778 by Thomas, 1st Earl of Bective, dominates all: a monolithic, ill-proportioned and completely inappropriate piece of stonework.

Within the churchyard there is an impressive round tower whose five windows looked out over the town's five gates. And there are four, possibly 11th-century, Celtic High Crosses (one virtually destroyed by Cromwell's troops) on which can be seen carvings of scenes from the Gospels.

Inside, in the old baptistry there is an excellent reproduction of the book of Kells; a disused gallery has also been converted into an exhibition area giving good information about the monastic history of the site. The stained glass is good Victorian, and there is an impressive early-18th-century monument to Thomas Taylour, a Privy Councillor.

Nearby: Kells, Co. Meath, St Colum Cille's House

KELLS, CO. MEATH
St Colum Cille's House

In a street adjacent to the Church of St Columba is a place that is equally strange. Squashed between modest residential houses, is St Colum Cille's House (St Columba's House).

It is not a house in the residential sense: it seems that it was probably a chapel built to house the saint's relics. It is also believed that the manuscripts of the 9th century Book of Kells were completed here.

The saint had originally been banished from Ireland for his crime of copying a book; he went to Iona, and only returned to Ireland when Iona was raided by the Vikings. He ingeniously got around the banishment by strapping sods of turf from Iona to the soles of his shoes, thus being able to claim that he was not actually setting foot on Irish soil.

There is a key available from the churchwarden to access the interior.

Nearby: Kells, Co. Meath, St Columba

KILKENNY
St Canice

Kilkenny's cathedral is a low, thickset building dating from the 13th century, whose lofty round tower – from an earlier religious site – watches over the town. It has a plain and simple appeal, especially inside, where the Early English style is prevalent.

The cathedral was built during the 13th century, and, in the early 14th century, suffered a common problem: the collapse of the central tower. Bishop Ledrede, who had also built

the impressive three-light east window, rebuilt it in the latter part of the
14th century to a more modest
height. The principal restoration was
carried out under Dean Vignoles, in
the 19th century, and it is rare to find
a Victorian restoration that has so
sensitively accommodated an earlier
medieval building.

The interior comprises a long nave
with side aisles, a central crossing,
north and south transepts, and a spacious chancel with side aisles to the
choir; the choir stalls are fine carved
copies of the choir stalls in Bruges
Cathedral. The stone vaulting of the
crossing is worth looking at: decorative rather than structural, it is a fine
piece of design. The south transept is
the burial place of the Lords of
Kilkenny Castle, the Butler family;
there is a fine 16th century tomb
bearing a double effigy of Piers and
Margaret Butler. Indeed, throughout
the cathedral there is a wealth of
interesting memorials. Tomb slabs
situated in the floor of the north aisle
are of special interest. The 'Cock on
the Pot' slab illustrates the legend of
the cock that was being cooked for
Judas's supper when it rose out of
the pot and crowed. Nearby are slabs
that bear the tools of trade of those
commemorated – the Weaver, the
Carpenter and the Cobbler.

The Chapter Room, in the chapel
off the south transept, is in complete
contrast to the rest of the cathedral.
Its outer walls are almost completely
glazed, creating a light airy space at
variance with the generally darker
cathedral interior. Outside, the
churchyard contains a Celtic High
Cross, and a pleasant jumble of tombstones through which to wander.

Nearby: Gowran, St Mary; Tullaherin,
Kilfane Church

The Butler tomb in the south transept

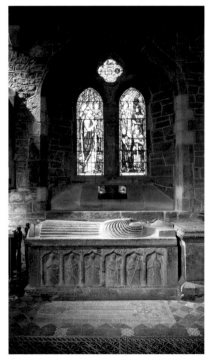

KILREE
Round Tower

This is an enigmatic place: a lofty round tower rises from a copse of beech and oak; within the shadowy and overgrown copse are a graveyard, and the ruins of an old church.

The round tower is some 90 feet high. The church is of the most simple two-cell plan, possibly a chapel dedicated to a saint: there is little evidence of any monastic building. Across a field to the west of the tower there is a much-weathered 9th-century High Cross. It bears five bosses on its west face, is covered with spiral motifs and cross-hatching, and there are faint traces of figurative carving, one of which depicts Daniel in the lion's den.

There is little indication as to the origin of this ancient and secluded place. It could be that it was related in some way to the nearby priory at Kells. The ground is still consecrated, and the occasional burial takes place here.

Nearby: Kells, Co. Kilkenny, Kells Priory

LOUGHINISLAND
Loughinisland Churches

This group of roofless churches, clustered on a rise overlooking Loughinisland Lake, is a true delight to visit. Its charm lies partly in the situation – it is surrounded by velvety pastureland – and partly in the way that ruination and a continued use of the surrounding grassy hillside as a burial ground combine past and present with an unselfconscious intimacy.

The surrounding graveyard contains some interesting stones: they range

from the poorest of crudely inscribed rough stone (possibly dating from the years of the Great Famine), to good examples of funerary masonry. Set down the hill a bit is a solid, 19th-century, beehive-shaped family vault.

Originally on an islet in the lake, the three tiny churches are now reached by a modern causeway. All are built from split rubble stone, with rough-dressed quoins. None is aligned the same: they jostle for space on the summit of the small hill. They have widely differing dates too: the Middle Church is thought to be of 13th-century origin; the North Church was built in the late 15th to early 16th century; and MacCartan's Chapel, the South Church, was built in the 17th century (Loughinisland was for 600 years the principal burial ground of the MacCartans, chiefs of Kinelarty). The South Church also contains an effigy of a human head set above the doorway, which looks to be older than the church. The North Church was used for both Protestant and Catholic worship until 1720, when the Protestant congregation decamped to a new church in nearby Seaforde, inconveniently taking the roof with them. It contains the oldest tombstone, set in the wall, with an inscription to a prudent gentleman of foresight which, when translated, reads, 'Maurice Burn lies covered by this pile of stones which, whilst living, he erected at his own expense'.

Nearby: Crossgar, Saul Church; Downpatrick, Down Cathedral; Downpatrick, Inch Abbey

THOMASTOWN
Jerpoint Abbey *OPW*

One could not find a place in Ireland that gives a more vivid impression of Cistercian life than Jerpoint Abbey. This is one of the monastic sites where a fine balance has been achieved between housing some items in a separate area, and leaving a wealth of carving and stonework in situ, thus enabling the visitor to more easily envisage the monastery as it was.

Jerpoint was founded in about 1160, and taken over by Cistercians from Baltinglass Abbey in 1180. It became a sizeable medieval town, which, by the 17th century, had all but disappeared.

The abbey is built to a conventional Cistercian plan: cruciform with nave, north and south transepts and chancel. Adjoining the south transept is the chapter house, which faces on to the extensive cloister garth, set to the south of the nave. At the extreme southern end of the garth are the vestigial remains of the kitchens, refectory and warming room. The cloister itself is impressive. Although the lean-to roof is long gone, the Romanesque supporting arcade has survived well; on the piers can be seen a variety of carvings of Butler knights, bishops and grotesque figures.

On the north wall of the chancel are faint traces of wall paintings depicting heraldic shields. Here too is an effigy, thought to be of the first abbot of Jerpoint, Felix O'Dullany. In two side chapels leading off the north transept are two 15th-century tombs, one bearing a carved stone panel of saints. There is a fine carving of St Christopher set in the wall of the north cloister range, while under the crossing is the superb tomb of Robert Walsh and Katherine Power. This dates from 1501, and the sculptor's name – Rory O'Tunney – can be made out on the stem of the cross. The south transept also has two side chapels, in one of which can be found a stone slab on which are carved two figures of 13th-century knights; opposite is a carved figure of an abbot.

Nearby: Graiguenamanagh, Duiske Abbey

THURLES
Holy Cross Abbey

This imposing former Cistercian abbey, on the banks of the river Suir, is a historical monument come back to life as a parish church. In October 1880 Holy Cross Abbey passed into the custody of the Commission of Public Works. In the 1960s a local initiative to restore and re-invest Holy Cross Abbey as a parish church culminated in the unanimous passing of the 'Holy Cross Abbey Bill 1969'. This made Holy Cross an exception to the 1869 Irish Church Act, which allowed the Church of Ireland Commissioners to transfer important churches and ecclesiastical buildings into state care, to be preserved as national monuments rather than places of worship, and, in 1975, the abbey once again opened its doors to the faithful.

The abbey had suffered setbacks in previous centuries. Founded by Cistercians from Monasteranenagh Abbey, the first 200 years were precarious: the abbey's survival was only assured by the arrival of a Norman benefactor, James Butler, 4th Earl of Ormond. During this period the abbey church acquired a new chancel, north and south transepts, the choir and the formidable tower. At the suppression, the monastery was closed, although a skeletal community of monks persisted until the 17th century, after which the abbey fell into ruins.

The original cellar and store and the monk's dormitory are now used as offices and a shop. Of the south cloister range, the site of the kitchen refectory, nothing now remains, but the extensive east range still contains the ruins

of the abbot's lodge and guest quarters, as well as the chapter house – entered through a doorway whose jambs and arch are rich with a curious repetitive rectangular motif.

In the abbey church itself, there is an air of tranquillity, although disconcertingly, when one enters through the west doorway, one finds oneself looking downhill. The whole nave slopes west–east at a considerable angle, following the underlying bedrock. The chancel contains elaborately carved sedilia, surmounted by an ornate stone canopy, and opposite is a carving of the Crucifixion. The stone vaulting of the crossing and

transepts is finely and intricately executed. The north transept contains an interesting, if very faint, mural depicting a hunting scene. It is one of only a few to date from the pre-Reformation period in Ireland.

Outside, to the east of the Abbot's lodge, is a tangle of ruined buildings that originally served pilgrims. The only jarring note is a suburban greenhouse-like housing for an outdoor altar, aesthetically at odds with the dignity of the abbey and monastery buildings.

Nearby: Freshford, Ballylarkin Abbey

TULLAHERIN
Kilfane Church

Kilfane is an obscure church, buried in the countryside some two miles from Tullaherin. Roofless, silent and shrouded by yews, it contains a unique Irish medieval antiquity.

Kilfane church is a late-14th- or

early-15th-century church, with an adjoining Norman tower house. It is thought that the site had a church founded by a contemporary of St Patrick. There are a number of interesting features to be seen: the consecration crosses on the walls by the west door, and on the north and south walls of the nave; and three ogee-headed doorways.

What dramatically commands one's attention, however, is a superb upright effigy, standing lonely and isolated against the north wall of the nave. This is Cantwell Fada, a Norman knight. Dressed in chain mail, partly covered by a surcoat, the knight holds his

shield – bearing the Cantwell heraldic device – in his left hand. His legs are crossed, which is believed by some to be a symbol of his having taken part in a crusade, and around his ankles are rowel-spurs, a feature that suggests the effigy to be of 14th-century origin. This is an exceptional piece of carving, all the more so as it stands out in all weathers. The setting is both dramatic and touching: one feels one should tarry there, keeping company with the knight.

Nearby: Gowran, St Mary; Kilkenny, St Canice

WATERFORD
Christ Church

Waterford has two cathedrals, both designed by the city's architect John Roberts, and about five minutes' walking distance from each other. Christ Church Cathedral is an outstanding neoclassical building, and contains the only remaining consistorial court in Ireland.

This finely proportioned cathedral stands on the site of a church built by Viking converts to Christianity at the beginning of the 11th century; it was superseded by a Norman building

until a modernising City Corporation decided that a new cathedral building would more accurately represent the spirit of 18th-century Waterford.

The decision was not without controversy, one opponent being the Bishop. But whatever was lost with the demolition (by gunpowder) of the Norman building, was more than adequately compensated for in John Roberts' new building. Its classical interior is light and finely proportioned, with outstanding stucco work

to the ceiling. The organ gallery is sited at the entrance to the nave, an unusual but striking arrangement.

The consistorial court is one of only a few remaining in Ireland: in it the Bishops would deal with such matters as intestacy, the issuing of wills and marriage licences, and contraventions of church law, such as blasphemy and sacrilege. Currently it is used as a choir room, and the visitor has to negotiate stacks of chairs to discover the detail.

The cathedral is a most uplifting building to visit, and is also the venue for an interesting annual programme of concerts and organ recitals.

Glossary

aisle parallel extensions to the side of the nave or choir, separated by an arcade of pillars

ambulatory an area for walking, particularly with reference to an apse or cloister

apse semicircular or polygonal recess at the eastern end of a church, usually containing the altar

arcade a series of arches supported by columns

arch spring the point from where an arch rises on a supporting column

aumbry a recess or cupboard used to house the communion bread and wine

ballflower a 14th century form of decoration consisting of a globular flower with incurved petals

barrel vaulting a roof formed of a single curve, either in stone or wood. Also known as a wagon vault

beakhead Norman stone ornamentation, not necessarily fashioned as a bird, but based on the shape of a bird's beak

bier a frame, sometimes with wheels, on which a coffin is placed prior to burial

blind arcade a series of arches applied to a wall as a form of decoration

boss a piece of ornamental carving covering the point where the ribs in a vault or ceiling meet

box pew a church pew enclosed by wooden partitions

broach spire a spire where the base is pyramidal in form

buttress a projecting stone support built against a wall, typically to counter outward thrust from overhead weight

campanile an Italianate bell tower

capital a broader and often carved section at the top of a pillar

cat-slide roof a deep roof whose angle eases nearer the bottom

chancel the part of a church containing the altar, usually reserved for clergy

chapel of ease a small subsidiary church used to accommodate an overflow from its parent church, or to cater for parishioners who live some distance from the church

choir stalls fixed seating for members of a choir or monks, usually within the chancel

cinquefoil five-lobed – or leaved – stone tracery, typically found in arches and window

clas Welsh term for an early form of monastic community

clerestory the upper part of a church containing a row of additional windows, usually above the nave

columbarium a space in which funeral urns are kept, and more archaically a dovecote

corbel table a projecting course of stones that support a parapet of cornice

corbels stone brackets that support the corbel table, often elaborately carved

crenellation battlements surmounting walls

crocket a small carved ornament, typically a bud or curled leaf, on the inclined side of a pinnacle or gable. A feature of Gothic architecture

cruciform a description applied to a church plan in the form of a cross

cupola a small rounded enclosing dome at the top a of circular structure

curvilinear a flowing style of stone tracery developing from the Geometric style, from the 14th century

dogtooth a late Norman/Early English form of stone ornamentation, usually used on

arches and tympanum: also known as nail-head

dripstone or hood mould a projecting stone moulding above an arch or window to deflect rainwater

early English the first period of English Gothic architecture, in which the rounded Norman arch was replaced by a pointed one

effigy a stone or marble carving of a human likeness, used on tombs and memorials

fan vault a set of concave ribs spreading out from a central point like the ribs of an opened umbrella. Typical of the English Perpendicular style

finial an ornamented top at the apex of a roof or pinnacle

flying buttress a pier that forms an arch with the wall that it is supporting

garth the open space enclosed by a cloister

geometric an angular style of tracery that developed from the Early English style

groined vault the intersection of two barrel vaulted roofs, usually without stone ribs

grotesques Romanesque carvings of people and animals in exaggerated or stylised form

hammer beam a short
wooden beam project-
ing from a wall to
support either a princi-
pal rafter or one end of an arch. A
double hammer beam is a short supporting wooden beam set on a lower
beam projecting from a wall

hatchment a large tablet, typically
diamond-shaped, bearing the coat
of arms of someone who has died,
displayed in their honour

hog back tomb a long ridged tombstone
used by the Vikings

iconostasis a screen bearing icons,
separating the sanctuary of
Orthodox churches from the nave

jambs the side post or column of a
doorway

Jesse tree a carved or stained-glass representation of the genealogy of Jesus,
in the form of a tree with Jesse at the
base and intermediate descendants on
branching scrolls of foliage

Jesse window a church window showing
Jesus' descent from Jesse, typically in
the form of a Jesse tree

keystone tapered stone used
to 'lock' an archway into
place

lancet windows slender Early
English window, coming
to a point at the centre of the arch

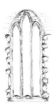

llan community of Celtic monks and
their families

lychgate a roofed gateway to a churchyard formerly used for sheltering a
coffin until the clergyman's arrival

misericord a ledge that projects from the
underside of a
hinged wooden
seat in the choir
stall, often ornately
carved

mounting block a set of stone steps set in
or adjacent to a churchyard, to allow
people to mount their horses more
easily

mullion a vertical bar between the panes
of glass in a window

narthex a distinct area at the western
entrance of a church. Derives from
early Christian churches

nave the central part of church used by
congregation

ogee a stone moulding with an s-shaped
profile

ogham Ancient British and Irish script of
20 characters

palladian in the neo-classical style of
Andrea Palladio, relating to the phase
of English architecture from 1715

parapet a low wall along the edge of a roof

parclose a screen or railing in a church
enclosing a tomb or altar or separating off a side chapel

parvise an upper room, often used for priest's accommodation, and later as a school or store room. Often found in the upper part of a church porch

paten a ceremonial plate on which bread is placed in the Eucharist

pediment the triangular upper part of the front of a building or doorway in clas- sical style, typically surmounting a portico of columns

pele tower a small square defensive tower of a kind built in the 16th century in the border counties of England and Scotland, often part of a church building

Perpendicular the latest stage of English Gothic church architec- ture, from the late 14th to mid 16th centuries and characterized by broad arches, elaborate fan vaulting, and large windows with vertical tracery

piscina shallow drained basin near the altar used for the washing of communion plate and chalices

plinth stone base of pillar

poppyhead refers to the carved top of a bench end  – derived from the Latin *puppis* – a figurehead, or from the French *poupée* – a doll

portico a roof supported by columns, typically the porch to a building

porticus a side chapel or extension, typical of an Anglo Saxon church, used for burials or storage of sacramental vessels

preaching cross a stone cross erected in a churchyard, under which travelling priests or friars would preach

pulpitum a screen, usually of stone, separating the crossing from the choir, usually bearing a pulpit, but also sometimes used as an organ loft

quatrefoil a design of four lobes or leaves used in architectural tracery, resembling a flower or four-leaf clover

reliquary an ornamented container for holy relics

reredos an ornamental screen behind an altar

respond a half-pillar attached to a wall, supporting an arch. Often found at the end of an arcade

retable the protective frame of a painting or relic above an altar

reticulated a style of decorated tracery characterized by circular shapes drawn at the top and bottom into ogees, resulting in a netlike framework

Rococo an elaborate ornamental late baroque style of decoration common in the 18th century

Romanesque a style of European architecture from 900–1200 AD, characterised by round heavy pillars,

and small round-headed windows
and doorways

rood crucifix or cross

rood loft elevated platform for the rood.
Latterly used for church musicians

rood screen a carved wooden or stone
screen supporting the rood loft, and
separating the nave and chancel

saddleback roof a tower roof shaped like a
gable

sanctuary the part of the church containing the high altar

sedilia carved stone
seating for clergy,
set in the south
wall of the chancel

sgraffito a form of
decoration made by scratching
through a surface to reveal a lower
layer of a contrasting colour

spandrel a triangular space between the
shoulders of adjoining arches and the
ceiling above

splay the difference in width between
one side of a window opening and
the other

spring the point from where an arch
rises from a supporting column

squint aperture cut through pillar or
wall to allow those with restricted
views to see the celebrant at the high
altar, also known as a hagioscope

stoup a stone basin containing Holy Water

string courses a prominent horizontal
band of stones projecting from a wall

tabernacle an ornamented receptacle for
the consecrated host; most commonly
found in Catholic and Orthodox
churches

taxatio a medieval form of property tax

tester or *sounding board* the wooden
acoustic backing and canopy to a
pulpit. Found commonly in churches
where the pulpit had become the
main focus of the service

tie beam a horizontal beam connecting
rafters or roof trusses

tracery ornamental stone openwork,
common in the upper part of a
Gothic window

transepts, transeptual the two 'arms' of a
cruciform church

transitional the architectural period when
Norman and Early English styles co-
existed

transoms the horizontal bars of a window

trefoil an ornamental design of three
rounded lobes like a clover leaf, typically used in stone tracery

triforium a gallery or arcade above the
arches of the nave, choir, and
transepts of a church

truss wooden support, usually part of a
framework

tympanum the normally decorated space
in a Norman doorway above the
doorway

voussoir a wedge-shaped or tapered
stone used in an archway

wagon roof a single and continuous
ceiled roof

Details of Organisations

Many churches featured in this book are available to visit because of the hard work of an organisation working to preserve them. Churches maintained by organisations have their abbreviations next to the church name. For more information about access to these churches please contact the organisation in question.

Churches Conservation Trust CCT
1 West Smithfield
London
EC1A 9EE
www.visitchurches.org.uk

Friends of Friendless Churches FOFC
St Ann's Vestry
2 Church Entry
London EC4V 5HB
www.friendsoffriendlesschurches.org.uk

Historic Chapels Trust HCT
St George's German Lutheran Church,
55 Alie Street,
London E1 8EB
www.hct.org.uk

Historic Scotland HC
Head Office, Historic Scotland
Longmore House
Salisbury Place
Edinburgh EH9 1SH
www.historic-scotland.gov.uk

The Office of Public Works OPW
51 St Stephen's Green
Dublin 2
Ireland
www.opw.ie

The Scottish Redundant Churches Trust
SRCT
4 Queen's Gardens
St Andrews
Fife KY16 9TA
www.srct.org.uk

Welsh Assembly Government Historic
Environment Service CADW
Welsh Assembly Government
Plas Carew
Unit 5/7 Cefn Coed
Parc Nantgarw
Cardiff
CF15 7QQ
www.cadw.wales.gov.uk

Index